THE
PASSOVER
HAGGADAH

Library of Congress Cataloging-in-Publication Data is on file.

ISBN-13: 978-1-57965-907-3

Design by Evi-O.Studio | Susan Le
Cover design by Kimberly Glyder
Artwork photographed by Yaakov Israel

Artisan books are available at special discounts when purchased in bulk for premiums
and sales promotions as well as for fund-raising or educational use. Special editions or book
excerpts also can be created to specification. For details, contact the Special Sales Director
at the address below, or send an e-mail to specialmarkets@workman.com.

For speaking engagements, contact speakersbureau@workman.com.

Published by Artisan
A division of Workman Publishing Company, Inc.
225 Varick Street
New York, NY 10014-4381
artisanbooks.com

Artisan is a registered trademark of Workman Publishing Co., Inc.

Printed in the United States on responsibly sourced paper

5 7 9 10 8 6 4

THE
PASSOVER
HAGGADAH

AN ANCIENT STORY
FOR MODERN TIMES

BROUGHT TO YOU BY
TABLET MAGAZINE

ARTISAN | NEW YORK

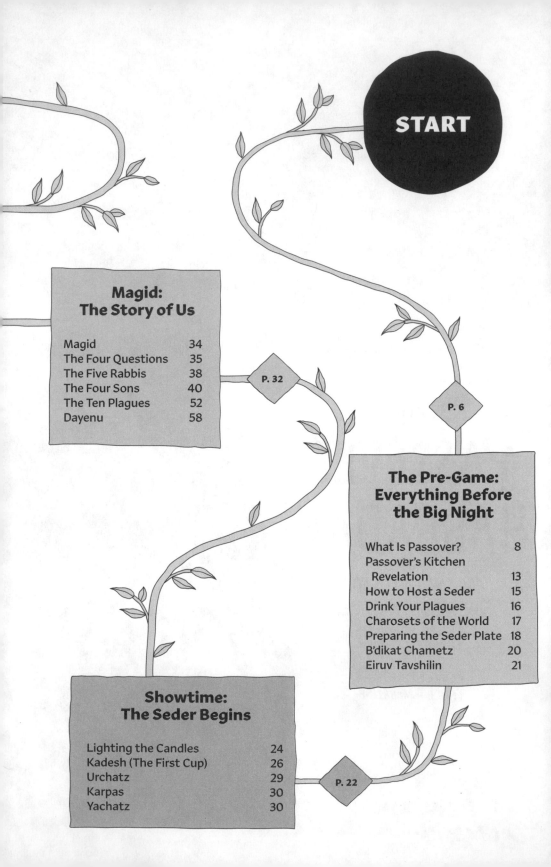

START

Magid: The Story of Us

P. 32

P. 6

The Pre-Game: Everything Before the Big Night

Showtime: The Seder Begins

P. 22

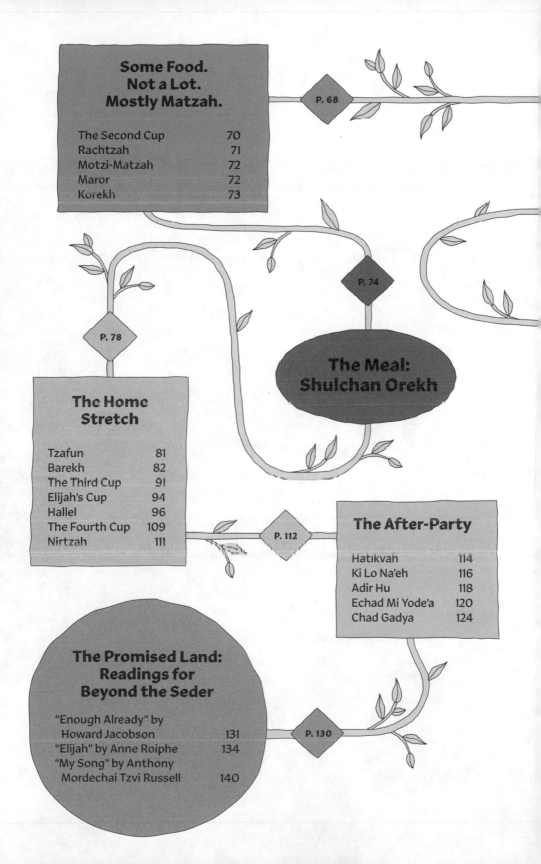

The Pre-Game

Everything Before
the Big Night

What Is Passover?

For generations, the Israelites were slaves in ancient Egypt under Pharaoh's tyranny. Passover marks their liberation and recounts, commemorates, and celebrates the story of their exodus, led by Moses, to freedom and to the Promised Land. Each generation is called to imagine themselves as if they *personally* experienced this— and so the holiday celebrates not only our historical liberation, but also our ongoing desire to remain spiritually, politically, and emotionally free.

Passover is one of the three harvest festivals—with Shavuot and Sukkot—in which the Jews of ancient Israel historically trekked to the Temple in Jerusalem to offer their sacrifices and first fruits. Since the Temple's destruction in 70 CE, we are no longer obliged to make the journey, but we still honor the memory of the harvest festival offerings by including a recitation of the Hallel, a prayer of thanksgiving.

The Hebrew name for Passover is *Pesach*, which comes from the Hebrew word "*pasach*," commonly translated as "passed over"—a reference to the Exodus passage that tells of God passing over the blood-marked doors of Jewish homes while slaying the firstborn sons of the Egyptians (we'll get to that later). Some scholars, however, suggest that a more accurate translation of the passage is that God "hovered over" the homes in question, signifying the Lord's eternal protection of the chosen people. We use "Pesach" and "Passover" interchangeably in this text.

Passover's two major requirements have to do with 1) abstaining from *chametz*, or unleavened bread, and 2) enacting what is known as a "Seder."

The word "*seder*" means "order" in Hebrew. Through Torah readings, *midrashim* (interpretations of biblical texts), songs, and discussion, Seder participants relive, as commanded, the events of Exodus, and hope for a rebuilt Temple in Jerusalem one day soon. For many, this is what makes Passover so special: its insistence that meaning and purpose come from telling (and fighting about, and embracing) our story—together.

Food as Magic

The first mention of this holiday is in the book of Leviticus—where it is referred to as the Feast of Unleavened Bread, owing to the fact that the Children of Israel hadn't enough time to let their dough rise before fleeing Egypt. Therefore, the avoidance of *chametz*—referring to all grain products that either have already been fermented (bread, cake, some alcoholic beverages) or can cause fermentation (yeast)—is at the heart of this experience.

Weeks before Passover, Jews embark on a serious spring cleaning. Although the *halacha*, or Jewish law, states no obligation to rid the home of any bit of *chametz* smaller than an olive, it has become customary to clean out every nook.

And while we all dream of pizza for eight unleavened days, some among us have an easier time: Sephardic and Mizrahi Jews—who descend from Spain, Portugal, North Africa, or the Middle East—customarily eat *kitniyot*, or legumes, during the holiday, which means they can have all the rice, beans, corn, peas, and lentils they want. Ashkenazi Jews, who hail from Eastern Europe, commonly avoid these delicious foods during the holiday.

Why Is This Haggadah Different from All Others?

The oldest surviving complete manuscript of the Haggadah dates to the tenth century, in a prayer book compiled by Saadia Gaon. But the text of the Haggadah was never fixed in one final form because after the Temple was destroyed, no rabbinic body existed that had authority over such matters. Instead, each local community developed its own text.

The one you are reading was produced in 2019 for the American Jewish community. Here and now, the Seder is the most popular Jewish ritual by a wide margin—far surpassing engagement in any other practice. Why? For starters, it is an experience that people of any background or education can find meaning in and enjoy. (You can invite your non-Jewish neighbor to fast with you on Yom Kippur, but it won't be that much fun for anyone involved.)

But there is something else, something deeply American about the Seder: its aggressive embrace of the future, while complicatedly holding fast to history. Passover is transcendent precisely because it manages to be both traditional—Jews read the same story that our ancestors have been reciting for millennia—and personal, with each of us making the Seder our own by incorporating our own interpretations and interests into the timeless tale of the exodus. Do you hate the idea that innocent Egyptians had to be killed in order for Jews to be liberated? Say so. Disgusted by the commandment to "blunt the teeth" of a young boy for the crime of phrasing a question in legitimately skeptical terms? Rant away! Challenge and engagement are, in fact, the very point of this experience—and what this document is designed to make us do.

We used the traditional text as a base and enriched it with questions, illustrations, and meditations on freedom, community, destiny, and other topics that are easier to discuss once you've started in on those obligatory four cups of wine.

Finally, a note about pronouns: Hebrew is a gendered language, and so we've used He/Him throughout, as it exists in the first Haggadah texts. Feel free to use whatever pronouns feel right to you.

We hope you'll find meaning here, but even more, we hope that you can make the Seder your own—indeed, that everyone around you can.

Passover's Kitchen Revelation: Cutting Down on Food Waste

In this postmodern age, Passover is, in part, about doing something hard—not eating what you're used to and what you sometimes desperately crave—perhaps to prepare us for the difficult work that liberation unfortunately requires. And while Passover is not formally the holiday during which we do the big accounting of our souls, many a rabbi urges us to "search for the meaning behind the mitzvah" of ridding our homes of *chametz*. Removing it "from our homes, our lives, our families, is a struggle between who we really are now and who we can be once we strip away all the trappings of self-importance," according to one source.

Reducing the amount of food we waste seems like a great place to start this process. After all, in our age of climate change and widespread food insecurity, those uneaten leftovers and that salad mix going limp in the fridge seem to encapsulate all the puffed-up arrogance so many commentators have ascribed to forbidden Passover food.

In this moment, what we are asked to do by our tradition is to enact and in a small way reexperience a communal decision to leave enslavement behind. Our ancestors, as they fled, didn't think, "This dough hasn't risen yet. Let's chuck it." They knew it was something valuable and that what they did with it could determine the success or failure of their journey through an infertile clime. In time, that decision came to define not only who they were but also who we might become in our own age, in this relatively prosperous era.

We're offered at this season a choice between an easier route—one involving the lush possibility of donuts but that leaves us unmoored from both our history and the world's current reality of hunger and melting ice—and a harder one. In addition to the traditional narrative and some brittle crackers, that path holds out to us a serious assessment of what we buy and consume, and perhaps a few fleeting moments of contact with the Divine.

If you look around in your pantry, who knows what you might find?

—Liz Galst

How to Host a Seder

Five Commandments for doing it just right:

① **BE A LEADER:** Tonight, it doesn't matter how much you know or how much you've read or how religious you are. If you're the Seder's leader, come prepared: Read the text in advance and know the general outline of the evening. But more than anything, your job is to help your guests feel comfortable. You may choose to assign portions of the Haggadah to specific people based on their sensibilities, or you may simply go around the table and take turns. Whatever it is, read the room.

② **GIVE YOUR GUESTS HOMEWORK:** A few days before the big night, send everyone a nice email. Tell them what they'll be having for dinner. Build up expectations. Send them a thought-provoking article, or ask them to prepare something of their own, like a short reading, a favorite quote, or anything else they could share around the table.

③ **FOOD IS YOUR FRIEND:** One of Passover's best features is the way that specialized foods are used for symbolism and imaginative power. Experiment with buying fresh horseradish this year, making a new charoset, or reviving your grandmother's favorite holiday dish. These all make for great conversation starters.

④ **KEEP THE KIDS HAPPY:** Got little ones running around? They need to be engaged. Hold a mini Seder with toys, have them create a Lego diorama for the table, make masks together for "Chad Gadya"—anything to keep 'em interested.

⑤ **WHEN MAKING YOUR INVITE LIST, BE BRAVE:** By the time we get to page 34's famous line, "Let all who are hungry come eat; let all in need come celebrate Pesach," it's already too late to answer the challenge. Do it now. Open your home and your table to someone new.

Drink Your Plagues
10 Deadly Cocktails

BOILS
Bumpy Eruption
*Cognac · crème de cassis ·
tequila · Cointreau*

HAIL
Hailfire & Brewski
White rum · ginger beer

LOCUSTS
Desert Swarm
Rum · gin

DARKNESS
Elysian Dream
Cognac · absinthe

**DEATH OF
THE FIRSTBORN**
Pharaoh's Lament
Sparkling wine · absinthe

BLOOD
Red Nile
Potato vodka

FROGS
Paris in April
*Cognac · Chartreuse
· Grand Marnier*

LICE
The Cockroach
Tequila · Sabra coffee liqueur

WILD BEASTS
Zion King
Brandy · gin

PESTILENCE
Buffalo
Fly Shooter
Potato vodka · arak

The night before the Seder, drop
one or two pomegranate seeds
in each square of an ice-cube tray.
When added to water glasses,
they'll look like drops of blood.

Charosets of the World

"Charoset" means "clay"—and though its consistency is meant to recall the mortar used by the Jews to build structures for the Egyptians during their enslavement, it's not meant to taste like it. In fact, there's no one recipe. Since Jews were scattered all over the world, they looked to their surrounding societies and agricultures for inspiration and created a mosaic of charosets, all different in ingredients but joined in a common injunction: Make it sticky and make it sweet.

NEW ORLEANS, USA
Apples + pecans + sweet wine + cinnamon

CALCUTTA, INDIA
Date molasses (*silan*) + walnuts

TASHKENT, UZBEKISTAN
Apples + walnuts + raisins + persimmons

VENICE, ITALY
Dates + chestnuts + raisins + orange juice

YEMEN
Dates + figs + raisins + walnuts + sesame seeds + ginger + cardamom + coriander + black pepper

ALEPPO, SYRIA
Dates + sweet wine + hazelnuts or walnuts

SURINAME, SOUTH AMERICA
Dried coconut + walnuts + raisins + apricots + pears

GREECE
Dates + currants + raisins + pine nuts + cinnamon + cloves

For charoset and cocktail recipes, go to tabletmag.com/haggadah.

MONTREAL, CANADA
Apples + walnuts + sweet wine + cinnamon + maple syrup

IRAN
Dates + raisins + walnuts + almonds + hazelnuts + vinegar + pomegranate juice + cardamom + cinnamon + ginger

Preparing the Seder Plate

CHAZERET
A second bitter herb, often Romaine lettuce. (No one really understands this one.)

CHAROSET
Everybody's favorite, it symbolizes the mortar the enslaved Israelites used in Egypt. It's a thick, sweet paste often made by mixing fruit, nuts, and sweet wine or juice.

SHANK BONE (Z'ROA)
A roasted bone symbolizes the Paschal sacrifice. Alternatively, any little bit of meat or bone will do, or even a blood-red beet.

ORANGE
Showing solidarity with LGBTQ Jews

CASHEWS
Support for the troops

BANANAS
Standing with refugees

Here is everything you'll need to assemble a traditional Seder plate—as well as some modern additions. Once your plate is ready, gather and cover three pieces of matzah. This way, when you break the middle piece for the *afikoman* (page 30), you'll still have two whole ones for Motzi-Matzah (page 72).

BITTER HERBS (MAROR)

Bitter herbs symbolize the bitterness of life in the house of bondage. Many use horseradish.

HARD-BOILED EGG (BEITZAH)

Another reminder of the Paschal sacrifice and an all-purpose symbol of the cycle of life.

GREEN VEGETABLE (KARPAS)

Karpas symbolizes spring. You can use parsley, celery, or even potato or onion.

Consider adding:

FAIR-TRADE CHOCOLATE

Demanding fair labor conditions in developing countries

OLIVES

Yearning for peace between Israelis and Palestinians

PINE CONES

Calling out for criminal justice reform

B'dikat Chametz

On the evening before the Seder, it's customary to search for any unleavened bread you may have forgotten around the house.

Follow these four easy steps:

(1) *Obtain a feather and a candle (or a flashlight—really, it's allowed!)*

(2) *Hide a few packages of **chametz** (traditionally, a few bread crumbs wrapped in newspaper or tinfoil) in different spots around the house.*

(3) *Invite children, friends, and relatives to join you in the search.*

(4) *Once all pieces have been discovered, say the following blessing:*

בְּרוּךְ אַתָּה יְהֹוָה אֱלֹהֵינוּ מֶלֶךְ הָעוֹלָם, אֲשֶׁר קִדְּשָׁנוּ בְּמִצְוֹתָיו וְצִוָּנוּ עַל בִּיעוּר חָמֵץ.

Barukh ata Adonai Eloheinu melekh ha'olam, asher kid'shanu b'mitzvotav v'tzivanu al bi'ur chametz.

Blessed are You, *HaShem*, our God, Ruler of the Universe, who has sanctified us with His commandments and given us the commandment of removing *chametz*.

---

*Immediately after the search has ended, disown the **chametz** by reciting the following:*

כָּל חֲמִירָא וַחֲמִיעָא דְּאִכָּא בִרְשׁוּתִי, דְּלָא חֲמִתֵּיה וּדְלָא בְעַרְתֵּיה וּדְלָא יְדַעְנָא לֵיהּ, לִבְטִיל וְלֶהֱוֵי הֶפְקֵר כְּעַפְרָא דְּאַרְעָא.

Kol chamira vachami'a d'ika virshuti, d'la chamiteih udla vi'arteih udla y'da'na leih, livtil v'lehevei hefkeir k'afra d'ar'a.

Let any *chametz* or leaven in my possession that I have neither seen, nor removed, nor known about be annulled and ownerless like dust.

---

*Early the next morning, all remaining **chametz** should be burned.*

After the burning, recite:

כָּל חֲמִירָא וַחֲמִיעָא דְּאִיכָּא בִרְשׁוּתִי, דַּחֲזִתֵּיה
וּדְלָא חֲזִתֵּיה, דַּחֲמִתֵּיה וּדְלָא חֲמִתֵּיה,
דְּבַעַרְתֵּיה וּדְלָא בְעַרְתֵּיה, לִבְטִיל וְלֶהֱוֵי הֶפְקֵר
כְּעַפְרָא דְּאַרְעָא.

Kol chamira vachami'a d'ika virshuti,
dachaziteih udla chaziteih, dachamiteih
udla chamiteih, d'vi'arteih udla vi'arteih,
livtil v'lehevei hefkeir k'afra d'ar'a.

Let any *chametz* or leaven in my possession—whether I have seen it or not, noticed it or not, removed it or not—be annulled and ownerless like dust.

Eiruv Tavshilin

If Pesach begins on a Wednesday night, preparing food on the holiday for the following Shabbat requires an eiruv tavshilin to be made and set aside. This consists of one cooked dish (usually a hard boiled egg) and one matzah. The following blessing is said:

בָּרוּךְ אַתָּה יְהֹוָה אֱלֹהֵינוּ מֶלֶךְ הָעוֹלָם, אֲשֶׁר
קִדְּשָׁנוּ בְּמִצְוֹתָיו וְצִוָּנוּ עַל מִצְוַת עֵרוּב.

Barukh ata Adonai Eloheinu melekh
ha'olam asher, kid'shanu b'mitzvotav
v'tzivanu al mitzvat eiruv.

Blessed are You, *HaShem*, our God, Ruler of the Universe, who has sanctified us with His commandments and given us the commandment of the *eiruv*.

בַּהֲדֵין עֵרוּבָא יְהֵא שָׁרֵא לָנָא לַאֲפוּיֵי וּלְבַשּׁוּלֵי
וּלְאַטְמוּנֵי וּלְאַדְלוּקֵי שְׁרָגָא וּלְמֶעְבַּד כָּל
צָרְכָנָא מִיּוֹמָא טָבָא לְשַׁבַּתָּא, לָנוּ וּלְכָל
יִשְׂרָאֵל הַדָּרִים בָּעִיר הַזֹּאת.

Bahadein eiruva y'hei sharei lana
la'afuyei ulvashulei ul'atmunei ul'adlukei
sh'raga ulme'bad kol tzorkhana miyoma
tava l'shabata, lanu ul'khol Yisra'eil
hadarim ba'ir hazot.

Through this *eiruv* may we and all Jews residing in this city be permitted to bake, cook, insulate, kindle a flame, prepare, and do anything otherwise necessary on Yom Tov for the sake of Shabbat.

Showtime

The Seder
Begins

Lighting the Candles

You'll need at least two candlesticks. (Some people like to add additional candles for each of their children.)

At sundown, light the candles and say the following blessing:

בָּרוּךְ אַתָּה יְהֹוָה אֱלֹהֵינוּ מֶלֶךְ הָעוֹלָם, אֲשֶׁר קִדְּשָׁנוּ בְּמִצְוֹתָיו וְצִוָּנוּ לְהַדְלִיק נֵר שֶׁל יוֹם טוֹב.

Barukh ata Adonai Eloheinu melekh ha'olam, asher kid'shanu b'mitzvotav v'tzivanu l'hadlik neir shel Yom Tov.

Blessed are You, *HaShem*, our God, Ruler of the Universe, who has sanctified us with His commandments and commanded us to kindle the Yom Tov light.

If it's Shabbat, read this instead:

בָּרוּךְ אַתָּה יְהֹוָה אֱלֹהֵינוּ מֶלֶךְ הָעוֹלָם, אֲשֶׁר קִדְּשָׁנוּ בְּמִצְוֹתָיו וְצִוָּנוּ לְהַדְלִיק נֵר שֶׁל שַׁבָּת וְשֶׁל יוֹם טוֹב.

Barukh ata Adonai Eloheinu melekh ha'olam, asher kid'shanu b'mitzvotav v'tzivanu l'hadlik neir shel Shabbat v'shel Yom Tov.

Blessed are You, *HaShem*, our God, Ruler of the Universe, who has sanctified us with His commandments and commanded us to kindle the Shabbat and Yom Tov light.

And then recite the **Shehecheyanu**, *which we say to mark holidays and other special occasions:*

בָּרוּךְ אַתָּה יְהֹוָה אֱלֹהֵינוּ מֶלֶךְ הָעוֹלָם, שֶׁהֶחֱיָנוּ וְקִיְּמָנוּ וְהִגִּיעָנוּ לַזְּמַן הַזֶּה.

Barukh ata Adonai Eloheinu melekh ha'olam, shehecheyanu v'kiy'manu v'higi'anu laz'man haze.

Blessed are You, *HaShem*, our God, Ruler of the Universe, who has granted us life, sustained us, and brought us to this moment.

Now for the evening's road map—a recitation (said or sung!) of the events that are about to transpire

Kadesh	*Blessing over the first cup of wine*	קַדֵּשׁ
Urchatz	*Washing of the hands*	וּרְחַץ
Karpas	*Blessing over the green vegetable*	כַּרְפַּס
Yachatz	*Break the middle matzah*	יַחַץ
Magid	*Tell the Passover story*	מַגִּיד
Rachtzah	*Wash the hands, with blessing*	רָחְצָה
Motzi-Matzah	*Blessings over the matzah*	מוֹצִיא-מַצָּה
Maror	*Blessing over the bitter herbs*	מָרוֹר
Korekh	*Eat the matzah sandwich*	כּוֹרֵךְ
Shulchan Orekh	*Eat the main meal*	שֻׁלְחָן עוֹרֵךְ
Tzafun	*Eat the afikoman*	צָפוּן
Barekh	*Blessings after the meal*	בָּרֵךְ
Hallel	*Sing songs of praise*	הַלֵּל
Nirtzah	*End of the Seder*	נִרְצָה

• KADESH •
(THE FIRST CUP)

"Kadesh" means "to consecrate." Let us begin, then, by setting this evening aside as blessed and special. Pour your first cup, take a deep breath, and relax: You'll be drinking pretty soon. After the final blessing, some people recline as they take that first swig of wine. Raise your cup and here we go.

If the Seder is on Friday night, read this first:

(בלחש:) וַיְהִי עֶרֶב וַיְהִי בֹקֶר

(Quietly:) Vayhi erev vayhi voker

יוֹם הַשִּׁשִּׁי. וַיְכֻלּוּ הַשָּׁמַיִם וְהָאָרֶץ וְכָל־צְבָאָם. וַיְכַל אֱלֹהִים בַּיּוֹם הַשְּׁבִיעִי מְלַאכְתּוֹ אֲשֶׁר עָשָׂה, וַיִּשְׁבֹּת בַּיּוֹם הַשְּׁבִיעִי מִכָּל מְלַאכְתּוֹ אֲשֶׁר עָשָׂה. וַיְבָרֶךְ אֱלֹהִים אֶת יוֹם הַשְּׁבִיעִי וַיְקַדֵּשׁ אוֹתוֹ, כִּי בוֹ שָׁבַת מִכָּל מְלַאכְתּוֹ אֲשֶׁר בָּרָא אֱלֹהִים לַעֲשׂוֹת.

Yom haShishi. Vaykhulu hashamayim v'ha'aretz v'khol tz'va'am. Vaykhal Elohim bayom hash'vi'i m'lakhto asher asa, vayishbot bayom hash'vi'i mikol m'lakhto asher asa. Vayvarekh Elohim et yom hash'vi'i vaykadesh oto, ki vo shavat mikol m'lakhto asher bara Elohim la'asot.

(Quietly:) There was evening and there was morning—

The sixth day. The heavens and the earth were completed, and all their host. On the seventh day, God finished the work that He had done, and He ceased on the seventh day from all the work that He had done. God blessed the seventh day and sanctified it, because on it He ceased all of the work of creation that He had done.

בָּרוּךְ אַתָּה יְהֹוָה אֱלֹהֵינוּ מֶלֶךְ הָעוֹלָם, בּוֹרֵא פְּרִי הַגָּפֶן.

Barukh ata Adonai Eloheinu melekh ha'olam, borei p'ri hagafen.

בָּרוּךְ אַתָּה יְהֹוָה אֱלֹהֵינוּ מֶלֶךְ הָעוֹלָם, אֲשֶׁר בָּחַר בָּנוּ מִכָּל עָם וְרוֹמְמָנוּ מִכָּל לָשׁוֹן, וְקִדְּשָׁנוּ בְּמִצְוֹתָיו. וַתִּתֶּן לָנוּ יְהֹוָה אֱלֹהֵינוּ בְּאַהֲבָה (בשבת: שַׁבָּתוֹת לִמְנוּחָה וּ) מוֹעֲדִים לְשִׂמְחָה, חַגִּים וּזְמַנִּים לְשָׂשׂוֹן, (בשבת: אֶת יוֹם הַשַּׁבָּת הַזֶּה וְ) אֶת יוֹם חַג הַמַּצּוֹת הַזֶּה, זְמַן חֵרוּתֵנוּ, (בשבת: בְּאַהֲבָה) מִקְרָא קֹדֶשׁ, זֵכֶר לִיצִיאַת מִצְרָיִם. כִּי בָנוּ בָחַרְתָּ וְאוֹתָנוּ קִדַּשְׁתָּ מִכָּל הָעַמִּים, (בשבת: וְשַׁבָּת) וּמוֹעֲדֵי קָדְשֶׁךָ (בשבת: בְּאַהֲבָה וּבְרָצוֹן) בְּשִׂמְחָה וּבְשָׂשׂוֹן הִנְחַלְתָּנוּ.

Barukh ata Adonai Eloheinu melekh ha'olam, asher bachar banu mikol am v'rom'manu mikol lashon, v'kid'shanu b'mitzvotav. Vatitein lanu Adonai Eloheinu b'ahava (On Shabbat add: Shabbatot limnucha u-) mo'adim l'simcha, chagim uzmanim l'sason, (On Shabbat add: et yom haShabbat haze v') et yom Chag HaMatzahs haze, z'man cheiruteinu (On Shabbat add: b'ahava) mikra kodesh, zeikher litzi'at Mitzrayim. Ki vanu vacharta v'otanu kidashta mikol ha'amim, (On Shabbat add: v'Shabbat) uMo'adei kodshekha (On Shabbat add: b'ahava uvratzon) b'simcha uvsason hinchaltanu.

בָּרוּךְ אַתָּה יְהֹוָה, מְקַדֵּשׁ (בשבת: הַשַּׁבָּת וְ) יִשְׂרָאֵל וְהַזְּמַנִּים.

Barukh ata Adonai, m'kadesh (On Shabbat add: haShabbat v') Yisra'eil v'haz'manim.

Blessed are you, *HaShem*, our God, Ruler of the Universe, who creates the fruit of the vine.

Blessed are You, *HaShem*, our God, Ruler of the Universe, who has chosen us from among all the nations, raised us above all languages, and sanctified us with His commandments. You, *HaShem*, our God, have given us with love, (Shabbatot for rest,) seasons of happiness, festivals and special times of joy—(this Shabbat day, and) this Festival of Matzahs, our season of freedom, (in love,) "a holy assembly" in memory of the exodus from Egypt. For You have chosen and sanctified us from among all nations, and granted us (the Shabbat, and) holy times out of (love and favor,) happiness and joy as an inheritance.

Blessed are You, *HaShem*, who sanctifies (the Shabbat,) Israel, and the festive seasons.

Is it Saturday night? If yes, there are just two more paragraphs you need to read—the traditional Havdalah service, which sets apart Shabbat from the rest of the days of the week.

בָּרוּךְ אַתָּה יְהֹוָה אֱלֹהֵינוּ מֶלֶךְ הָעוֹלָם, בּוֹרֵא מְאוֹרֵי הָאֵשׁ.

Barukh ata Adonai Eloheinu melekh ha'olam, borei m'orei ha'eish.

בָּרוּךְ אַתָּה יְהֹוָה אֱלֹהֵינוּ מֶלֶךְ הָעוֹלָם, הַמַּבְדִּיל בֵּין קֹדֶשׁ לְחוֹל, בֵּין אוֹר לְחֹשֶׁךְ, בֵּין יִשְׂרָאֵל לָעַמִּים, בֵּין יוֹם הַשְּׁבִיעִי לְשֵׁשֶׁת יְמֵי הַמַּעֲשֶׂה. בֵּין קְדֻשַּׁת שַׁבָּת לִקְדֻשַּׁת יוֹם טוֹב הִבְדַּלְתָּ, וְאֶת יוֹם הַשְּׁבִיעִי מִשֵּׁשֶׁת יְמֵי הַמַּעֲשֶׂה קִדַּשְׁתָּ. הִבְדַּלְתָּ וְקִדַּשְׁתָּ אֶת עַמְּךָ יִשְׂרָאֵל בִּקְדֻשָּׁתֶךָ.

Barukh ata Adonai Eloheinu melekh ha'olam, hamavdil bein kodesh l'chol, bein or l'choshekh, bein Yisra'eil la'amim, bein yom hash'vi'i l'sheishet y'mei hama'aseh. Bein k'dushat Shabbat likdushat Yom Tov hivdalta, v'et yom hash'vi'i misheishet y'mei hama'ase kidashta. Hivdalta v'kidashta et am'kha Yisra'eil bikdushatekha.

בָּרוּךְ אַתָּה יְהֹוָה, הַמַּבְדִּיל בֵּין קֹדֶשׁ לְקֹדֶשׁ.

Barukh ata Adonai, hamavdil bein kodesh l'kodesh.

Blessed are You, *HaShem*, our God, Ruler of the Universe, who creates the light of the fire.

Blessed are You, *HaShem*, our God, Ruler of the Universe, who distinguishes between the holy and the ordinary, between light and darkness, between Israel and the nations, between the seventh day and the six working days. You have distinguished between the holiness of Shabbat and the holiness of Yom Tov, and You have sanctified the seventh day above the six working days. You have distinguished and sanctified Your people Israel with Your holiness.

Blessed are You, *HaShem*, who distinguishes between degrees of holiness.

And now recite the final blessing, **Shehecheyanu:**

בָּרוּךְ אַתָּה יְהֹוָה אֱלֹהֵינוּ מֶלֶךְ הָעוֹלָם, שֶׁהֶחֱיָנוּ
וְקִיְּמָנוּ וְהִגִּיעָנוּ לַזְּמַן הַזֶּה.

Barukh ata Adonai Eloheinu melekh ha'olam, shehecheyanu v'kiy'manu v'higi'anu laz'man haze.

Blessed are You, *HaShem*, our God, Ruler of the Universe, who has granted us life, sustained us, and brought us to this moment.

Take a big sip of that wine (some do so while leaning to the left): The first cup is yours to enjoy.

Urchatz

"Urchatz" means "to wash," in this case, your hands. Take a moment to think about the special meal you're about to enjoy and the people you're fortunate to celebrate it with.

You don't have to do this in any ritualistic way, though some people use a special cup designed for just this purpose.

Karpas

Now we take a fruit of the earth—parsley, celery, boiled potato, raw onion, or anything else that tickles your fancy—and dip it in salt water. Some say the salt water symbolizes the tears of the enslaved Israelites. One lesser-known explanation says that this custom evokes the memory of Joseph's colorful coat being dipped in blood by his brothers. Either way, most sages agree that it's a pretty cool way to start a festive meal, as it prompts the younger folks around the table to ask why we're doing such strange things—the answer to which is, literally, the Haggadah.

As you dip, recite the following blessing:

בָּרוּךְ אַתָּה יְהֹוָה אֱלֹהֵינוּ מֶלֶךְ הָעוֹלָם, בּוֹרֵא פְּרִי הָאֲדָמָה.

Barukh ata Adonai Eloheinu melekh ha'olam, borei p'ri ha'adama.

Blessed are you, *HaShem*, our God, Ruler of the Universe, who creates the fruit of the earth.

Yachatz

Take the middle matzah from the pile on your table and break it into two, so that one piece is larger than the other. Put the smaller piece back on the table; you'll be using it soon enough. Take the larger piece, wrap it in a napkin (or a dedicated *afikoman* bag if you're fancy), and, when the kids aren't looking, hide it somewhere. Before the meal is over, they'll have to look for it, and whoever finds it gets to trade it in for candy, small gifts, or a little cash to sweeten the deal.

And now, we are ready to tell our story.

Magid

The Story
of Us

Magid

Uncover your matzah, raise the Seder plate, and jump in:

הָא לַחְמָא עַנְיָא דִּי אֲכָלוּ אֲבָהָתָנָא בְּאַרְעָא דְמִצְרָיִם. כָּל דִּכְפִין יֵיתֵי וְיֵיכֹל, כָּל דִצְרִיךְ יֵיתֵי וְיִפְסַח. הָשַׁתָּא הָכָא, לְשָׁנָה הַבָּאָה בְּאַרְעָא דְיִשְׂרָאֵל. הָשַׁתָּא עַבְדֵי, לְשָׁנָה הַבָּאָה בְּנֵי חוֹרִין.

Ha lachma anya di akhalu avahatana b'ar'a d'Mitzrayim. Kol dikhfin yeitei v'yeikhol, kol ditzrikh yeitei v'yifsach. Hashata hakha, l'shana haba'a b'ar'a d'Yisra'eil. Hashata avdei, l'shana haba'a b'nei chorin.

This is the bread of affliction that our ancestors ate in the land of Egypt. Let all who are hungry come eat; let all in need come celebrate Pesach. Now we are here; next year may we be in the Land of Israel. Now we are slaves; next year may we be free.

Refill your wineglass, but don't drink yet.

Can you remember a time you yourself went from hardship to great light and freedom?

The Four Questions

The youngest present around the table should now stand up and recite the evening's most famous song:

מַה נִּשְׁתַּנָּה הַלַּיְלָה הַזֶּה מִכָּל הַלֵּילוֹת?

1 שֶׁבְּכָל הַלֵּילוֹת אָנוּ אוֹכְלִין חָמֵץ וּמַצָּה— הַלַּיְלָה הַזֶּה כֻּלּוֹ מַצָּה.

2 שֶׁבְּכָל הַלֵּילוֹת אָנוּ אוֹכְלִין שְׁאָר יְרָקוֹת— הַלַּיְלָה הַזֶּה (כֻּלּוֹ) מָרוֹר.

3 שֶׁבְּכָל הַלֵּילוֹת אֵין אָנוּ מַטְבִּילִין אֲפִילוּ פַּעַם אֶחָת—הַלַּיְלָה הַזֶּה שְׁתֵּי פְעָמִים.

4 שֶׁבְּכָל הַלֵּילוֹת אָנוּ אוֹכְלִין בֵּין יוֹשְׁבִין וּבֵין מְסֻבִּין—הַלַּיְלָה הַזֶּה כֻּלָּנוּ מְסֻבִּין.

How is tonight different from all other nights?

1 On all other nights we eat leavened bread and matzah; tonight—only matzah.

2 On all other nights we eat other vegetables; tonight—only bitter herbs.

3 On all other nights, we don't dip our food at all; tonight—we dip twice.

4 On all other nights, we eat sitting or reclining; tonight—everyone reclines.

Ma nishtana halaila haze mikol haleilot?

1 Sheb'khol haleilot anu okh'lin chametz umatzah—halaila haze kulo matzah.

2 Sheb'khol haleilot anu okh'lin sh'ar y'rakot—halaila haze (kulo) maror.

3 Sheb'khol haleilot ein anu matbilin afilu pa'am echat—halaila haze sh'tei f'amim.

4 Sheb'khol haleilot anu okh'lin bein yoshvin uvein m'subin—halaila haze kulanu m'subin.

After reciting the four questions, we read the answer. Some families ask the oldest person present to recite this; others sing it all together.

עֲבָדִים הָיִינוּ לְפַרְעֹה בְּמִצְרַיִם, וַיּוֹצִיאֵנוּ יְהֹוָה אֱלֹהֵינוּ מִשָּׁם בְּיָד חֲזָקָה וּבִזְרֹעַ נְטוּיָה. וְאִלּוּ לֹא הוֹצִיא הַקָּדוֹשׁ בָּרוּךְ הוּא אֶת אֲבוֹתֵינוּ מִמִּצְרַיִם, הֲרֵי אָנוּ וּבָנֵינוּ וּבְנֵי בָנֵינוּ מְשֻׁעְבָּדִים הָיִינוּ לְפַרְעֹה בְּמִצְרַיִם. וַאֲפִילוּ כֻּלָּנוּ חֲכָמִים, כֻּלָּנוּ נְבוֹנִים, כֻּלָּנוּ זְקֵנִים, כֻּלָּנוּ יוֹדְעִים אֶת הַתּוֹרָה, מִצְוָה עָלֵינוּ לְסַפֵּר בִּיצִיאַת מִצְרָיִם. וְכָל הַמַּרְבֶּה לְסַפֵּר בִּיצִיאַת מִצְרַיִם הֲרֵי זֶה מְשֻׁבָּח.

Avadim hayinu l'Far'o b'Mitzrayim, vayotzi'einu Adonai Eloheinu misham b'yad chazaka uvizro'a n'tuya. V'ilu lo hotzi HaKadosh Barukh Hu et avoteinu miMitzrayim, harei anu uvaneinu uvnei vaneinu m'shu'badim hayinu l'Far'o b'Mitzrayim. V'afilu kulanu chakhamim, kulanu n'vonim, kulanu z'keinim, kulanu yod'im et haTora, mitzva aleinu l'sapeir bitzi'at Mitzrayim. V'khol hamarbe l'sapeir bitzi'at Mitzrayim harei ze m'shubach.

We were Pharaoh's slaves in Egypt, and *HaShem*, our God, took us out of there with a mighty hand and an outstretched arm. But had the Holy One not taken our ancestors out of Egypt, we and our children and our children's children would have remained enslaved to Pharaoh in Egypt. Even if we are all sages, all wise, all experienced, all knowledgeable about the Torah, we all must tell the story of the exodus from Egypt. And the more one tells about the exodus from Egypt, the more they deserve praise.

The Seder as Therapy

Passover, more than any other Jewish holiday, is the apotheosis—the ne plus ultra—of using remembrance as a way of fortifying tribal identity. The symbols of the holiday, gathered together on the Seder plate, all hearken back to our escape thousands of years ago from slavery to liberation, but they are also meant to speak to us in the here and now. We read aloud of our travails—and of the dire punishments visited on our Egyptian oppressors by an all-powerful and vengeful God—with the intention of reexperiencing both the dread of oppression and the exhilaration of freedom. In contemporary terms, the Haggadah can be seen as both a trauma narrative, filled with the psychic repetition that trauma produces, and a story of redemption, shot through with joy and song.

—*Daphne Merkin*

The Five Rabbis

These five Talmudic Sages weren't just random men. They were the wisest rabbis in the period directly following the destruction of the Second Temple in 70 CE. And this nocturnal meeting we read about here wasn't just a leisurely Seder; it might well have been a discussion about how to continue to sustain Judaism now that its beating heart, the Temple in Jerusalem, was no more.

If nothing else, we should learn from these men that even in the shadow of great tragedy, faith and friendship always find the way forward.

מַעֲשֶׂה בְּרַבִּי אֱלִיעֶזֶר וְרַבִּי יְהוֹשֻׁעַ וְרַבִּי אֶלְעָזָר בֶּן עֲזַרְיָה וְרַבִּי עֲקִיבָא וְרַבִּי טַרְפוֹן שֶׁהָיוּ מְסֻבִּין בִּבְנֵי בְרַק, וְהָיוּ מְסַפְּרִים בִּיצִיאַת מִצְרַיִם כָּל אוֹתוֹ הַלַּיְלָה, עַד שֶׁבָּאוּ תַלְמִידֵיהֶם וְאָמְרוּ לָהֶם: רַבּוֹתֵינוּ, הִגִּיעַ זְמַן קְרִיאַת שְׁמַע שֶׁל שַׁחֲרִית.

Ma'ase b'Rabi Eliezer v'Rabi Y'hoshu'a v'Rabi Elazar ben Azarya v'Rabi Akiva v'Rabi Tarfon shehayu m'subin biVnei V'rak, v'hayu m'sap'rim bitzi'at Mitzrayim kol oto halaila, ad sheba'u talmideihem v'am'ru lahem: Raboteinu, higi'a z'man k'ri'at Sh'ma shel Shacharit.

It once happened that Rabbi Eliezer, Rabbi Yehoshua, Rabbi Elazar ben Azariah, Rabbi Akiva, and Rabbi Tarfon were reclining in Bnei Brak and telling the story of the exodus from Egypt that whole night, until their students came and said to them, "Our teachers, the time has come to recite the morning *Shema*."

אָמַר רַבִּי אֶלְעָזָר בֶּן עֲזַרְיָה: הֲרֵי אֲנִי כְּבֶן שִׁבְעִים שָׁנָה וְלֹא זָכִיתִי שֶׁתֵּאָמֵר יְצִיאַת מִצְרַיִם בַּלֵּילוֹת עַד שֶׁדְּרָשָׁהּ בֶּן זוֹמָא, שֶׁנֶּאֱמַר: "לְמַעַן תִּזְכֹּר אֶת יוֹם צֵאתְךָ מֵאֶרֶץ מִצְרַיִם כֹּל יְמֵי חַיֶּיךָ." יְמֵי חַיֶּיךָ—הַיָּמִים. כֹּל יְמֵי חַיֶּיךָ—הַלֵּילוֹת. וַחֲכָמִים אוֹמְרִים: יְמֵי חַיֶּיךָ—הָעוֹלָם הַזֶּה. כֹּל יְמֵי חַיֶּיךָ—לְהָבִיא לִימוֹת הַמָּשִׁיחַ.

Amar Rabi Elazar ben Azarya: Harei ani k'ven shiv'im shana v'lo zakhiti shetei'ameir y'tzi'at Mitzrayim baleilot ad shed'rashah Ben Zoma, shene'emar: "L'ma'an tizkor et yom tzeit'kha me'eretz Mitzrayim kol y'mei chayekha." Y'mei chayekha—hayamim. Kol y'mei chayekha—haleilot. Vachakhamim om'rim: Y'mei chayekha—ha'olam hazeh. Kol y'mei chayekha—l'havi limot haMashi'ach.

Rabbi Elazar ben Azariah said: "I am like a man of seventy years yet I couldn't fathom why the story of the exodus from Egypt is mentioned nightly until Ben Zoma expounded it. For it says, 'In order that you remember the day you left the land of Egypt all the days of your life': 'the days of your life'—by day; '*all* the days of your life'—at night." But the Sages say, "'the days of your life'—in this world; '*all* the days of your life'—to include the messianic era."

If you could elect a sixth rabbi, who would it be? Whose ideas about Judaism do you respect?

בָּרוּךְ הַמָּקוֹם, בָּרוּךְ הוּא, בָּרוּךְ שֶׁנָּתַן תּוֹרָה לְעַמּוֹ יִשְׂרָאֵל, בָּרוּךְ הוּא.

Barukh HaMakom, barukh Hu, barukh shenatan Tora l'amo Yisra'eil, barukh Hu.

כְּנֶגֶד אַרְבָּעָה בָנִים דִּבְּרָה תוֹרָה: אֶחָד חָכָם, וְאֶחָד רָשָׁע, וְאֶחָד תָּם, וְאֶחָד שֶׁאֵינוֹ יוֹדֵעַ לִשְׁאוֹל.

K'neged arba'a vanim dib'ra Torah: Echad chakham, v'echad rasha, v'echad tam, v'echad she'eino yode'a lish'ol.

Blessed is God, Blessed is He; Blessed is the One who gave the Torah to His people Israel, Blessed is He.

The Torah speaks of four children: one who is wise, one who is wicked, one who is simple, and one who does not know how to ask.

The Four Sons

Having faith is hard. The story of Passover is all about magnificent and highly unlikely miracles, and while some of us take them at face value, others may have a difficult time believing that all of this ever went down.

Having faith is hard. The Haggadah, in its wisdom, foresees all possible reactions and teaches us that there are four types of people in this world, represented here by the Four Sons:

חָכָם מָה הוּא אוֹמֵר? "מָה הָעֵדֹת וְהַחֻקִּים וְהַמִּשְׁפָּטִים אֲשֶׁר צִוָּה יְהֹוָה אֱלֹהֵינוּ אֶתְכֶם." וְאַף אַתָּה אֱמָר לוֹ כְּהִלְכוֹת הַפֶּסַח, אֵין מַפְטִירִין אַחַר הַפֶּסַח אֲפִיקוֹמָן.

Chakham ma hu omeir? "Ma ha'eidot v'hachukim v'hamishpatim asher tziva Adonai Eloheinu etkhem." V'af ata emor lo k'hilkhot haPesach, ein maftirin achar haPesach afikoman.

What does the Wise Child say? "What are these testimonies, laws, and judgments that *HaShem*, our God, commanded you?" So you tell him the laws of the Pesach sacrifice, that we may not eat an *afikoman* after the Pesach sacrifice.

רָשָׁע מָה הוּא אוֹמֵר? "מָה הָעֲבוֹדָה הַזֹּאת לָכֶם." לָכֶם—וְלֹא לוֹ. וּלְפִי שֶׁהוֹצִיא אֶת עַצְמוֹ מִן הַכְּלָל כָּפַר בְּעִקָּר. וְאַף אַתָּה הַקְהֵה אֶת שִׁנָּיו וֶאֱמֹר לוֹ: "בַּעֲבוּר זֶה עָשָׂה יְהֹוָה לִי בְּצֵאתִי מִמִּצְרָיִם." לִי—וְלֹא לוֹ. אִלּוּ הָיָה שָׁם, לֹא הָיָה נִגְאָל.

Rasha ma hu omeir? "Ma ha'avoda hazot lakhem." Lakhem—v'lo lo. Ulfi shehotzi et atzmo min hak'lal kafar b'ikar. V'af ata hakhei et shinav ve'emor lo: "Ba'avur ze asa Adonai li b'tzeiti miMitzrayim." Li—v'lo lo. Ilu haya sham, lo haya nig'al.

What does the Wicked Child say? "What is this divine service of yours?" "Yours"—not his. Since he has excluded himself from the community, he has denied a fundamental principle [of Judaism]. So you blunt his teeth and tell him, "Because of this, *HaShem* did so for me when I left Egypt." "For me"—not for him; had he been there, he would not have been redeemed.

תָּם מָה הוּא אוֹמֵר? "מַה זֹּאת." וְאָמַרְתָּ אֵלָיו, "בְּחֹזֶק יָד הוֹצִיאָנוּ יְהֹוָה מִמִּצְרַיִם מִבֵּית עֲבָדִים."

Tam ma hu omeir? "Ma zot." V'amarta eilav, "B'chozek yad hotzi'anu Adonai mi Mitzrayim mibeit avadim."

What does the Simple Child say? "What is this?" You tell him, "With a mighty hand, *HaShem* took us out of Egypt, from the house of bondage."

וְשֶׁאֵינוֹ יוֹדֵעַ לִשְׁאוֹל אַתְּ פְּתַח לוֹ, שֶׁנֶּאֱמַר: "וְהִגַּדְתָּ לְבִנְךָ בַּיּוֹם הַהוּא לֵאמֹר, בַּעֲבוּר זֶה עָשָׂה יְהֹוָה לִי בְּצֵאתִי מִמִּצְרָיִם."

V'she'eino yode'a lish'ol at p'tach lo, shene'emar: "V'higad'ta l'vinkha bayom hahu leimor, ba'avur ze asa Adonai li b'tzeiti miMitzrayim."

As for the child who does not know how to ask, you initiate the conversation, as it says: "And you will tell your child on that day, saying: 'Because of this, *HaShem* did so for me when I left Egypt.'"

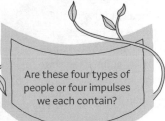

Are these four types of people or four impulses we each contain?

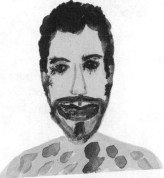

The Four Daughters

The Wise Ones Listen

The Wise Child is the kid who asks exactly the questions adults want to hear, like "Would you please explain the laws and customs of the Seder? I can't wait to hear all about it!" But to be wise is not, necessarily, to be a suck-up or a nerd. As Pirkei Avot, a compilation of ethical teachings, would have it, "Who is wise? The person who learns from all people." Someone is wise, then, when she knows that however much she does know, there is virtually no end to all that she doesn't. And that universe of possibility humbles and excites her at the same time.

—*Jordana Horn Gordon*

The Wicked Daughter's Still Here

The Wicked One, she is for all of us who can't easily slip inside the language of belonging; who can't uphold dogma and rules without critical inquiry; who recognize that it's not always wise to accept every answer; who have grappled enough to know that belief is no simple story; who have learned how, and why, to ask. The Wicked One, she is for all of us who still come to this Seder table but are tired of endless apologetics and obfuscation; she is for all of us who still care but no longer believe. This Wicked One is perhaps as uncomfortable on the page as we are sometimes around this table. But she remains there nonetheless, a reminder for every generation that shutting down a question is not the same thing as giving an answer.

—*Tova Mirvis*

We're not living in biblical times any longer, and we are long overdue to hear from the daughters. Below, four writers imagine female responses to the traditional archetypes of the Four Sons.

The Simple Life

All I did was ask what was going on at the Seder. When did it become a crime to admit there's something you don't know? Indeed, in a world where men portray complexity as sophistication and conflict as a sign of strength, isn't the purest impulse to be curious, modest, and genuine?

—*Stephanie Butnick*

No Further Questions

It has always struck me as unfair: Why on earth would you judge a child who did not "know enough to ask"? Isn't that the fault of his or her parents, educators, community?

I was that daughter who never investigated the charred egg, blinding *maror*, or why we recline; I was never told I could. No one debated the Haggadah; we just recited it. No one told me, "This story is yours, too; kick the tires."

The rabbis hammer home the Seder's core purpose: spark kids' inquiry, put strange objects in their sight—a lamb's limb, wet parsley, corrugated carbs—so that the children remain off-balance, absorbed. If they're curious, they'll stay awake. How shabby that the rabbis then denigrate the very kids they claim to want to coax out.

Talmud says we should answer the child who doesn't know enough to ask by "opening up" the conversation. I finally learned to crack it open for myself, and only wish I'd started before age forty. At least I can hope my own children will never be the fourth kid.

—*Abigail Pogrebin*

יָכוֹל מֵרֹאשׁ חֹדֶשׁ? תַּלְמוּד לוֹמַר, "בַּיּוֹם הַהוּא." אִי בַּיּוֹם הַהוּא, יָכוֹל מִבְּעוֹד יוֹם? תַּלְמוּד לוֹמַר, "בַּעֲבוּר זֶה"—בַּעֲבוּר זֶה לֹא אָמַרְתִּי אֶלָּא בְּשָׁעָה שֶׁיֵּשׁ מַצָּה וּמָרוֹר מֻנָּחִים לְפָנֶיךָ.

Yakhol meRosh Chodesh? Talmud lomar, "bayom hahu." I bayom hahu, yakhol mib'od yom? Talmud lomar, "ba'avur ze"—ba'avur ze lo amarti ela b'sha'a sheyesh matzah umaror munachim l'fanekha.

Perhaps [we should discuss the exodus] from the beginning of the month [of Nisan]? The verse teaches, "On that day." If "on that day," perhaps while it is still daytime? The verse teaches, "for the sake of *this*"—only when you have matzah and *maror* in front of you.

מִתְּחִלָּה עוֹבְדֵי עֲבוֹדָה זָרָה הָיוּ אֲבוֹתֵינוּ, וְעַכְשָׁיו קֵרְבָנוּ הַמָּקוֹם לַעֲבוֹדָתוֹ, שֶׁנֶּאֱמַר: "וַיֹּאמֶר יְהוֹשֻׁעַ אֶל כָּל הָעָם, כֹּה אָמַר יְהוָה אֱלֹהֵי יִשְׂרָאֵל, בְּעֵבֶר הַנָּהָר יָשְׁבוּ אֲבוֹתֵיכֶם מֵעוֹלָם, תֶּרַח אֲבִי אַבְרָהָם וַאֲבִי נָחוֹר, וַיַּעַבְדוּ אֱלֹהִים אֲחֵרִים. וָאֶקַּח אֶת אֲבִיכֶם אֶת אַבְרָהָם מֵעֵבֶר הַנָּהָר וָאוֹלֵךְ אוֹתוֹ בְּכָל אֶרֶץ כְּנָעַן, וָאַרְבֶּה אֶת זַרְעוֹ וָאֶתֶּן לוֹ אֶת יִצְחָק. וָאֶתֵּן לְיִצְחָק אֶת יַעֲקֹב וְאֶת עֵשָׂו. וָאֶתֵּן לְעֵשָׂו אֶת־הַר שֵׂעִיר לָרֶשֶׁת אוֹתוֹ, וְיַעֲקֹב וּבָנָיו יָרְדוּ מִצְרָיִם."

Mit'chila ov'dei avoda zara hayu avoteinu, v'akhshav keir'vanu haMakom la'avodato, shene'emar: "Vayomer Y'hoshu'a el kol ha'am, ko amar Adonai Elohei Yisra'eil, b'eiver hanahar yash'vu avoteikhem mei'olam, Terach avi Avraham va'avi Nachor, vaya'avdu Elohim acheirim. Va'ekach et avikhem et Avraham mei'ever hanahar va'oleikh oto b'khol eretz K'na'an, va'arbe et zar'o va'etein lo et Yitzchak. Va'etein l'Yitzchak et Ya'akov v'et Eisav. Va'etein l'Eisav et Har Sei'ir lareshet oto, v'Ya'akov uvanav yar'du Mitzrayim."

Originally, our ancestors worshipped idols. But now, God has brought us to His worship, as it is stated, "Joshua said to the entire people: 'So said *HaShem*, God of Israel: Your ancestors, Terach the father of Abraham and the father of Nachor, dwelled across the river from time immemorial and worshipped other gods. I took your father, Abraham, from across the river and had him walk throughout the entire land of Canaan. I increased his offspring and gave him Isaac. To Isaac I gave his sons Jacob and Esau. To Esau I gave Mount Seir as an inheritance, but Jacob and his sons went down to Egypt.'"

LEAPFROG

If you'd like to jump ahead, the next big moment is the Ten Plagues (page 52).

בָּרוּךְ שׁוֹמֵר הַבְטָחָתוֹ לְיִשְׂרָאֵל, בָּרוּךְ הוּא. שֶׁהַקָּדוֹשׁ בָּרוּךְ הוּא חִשַּׁב אֶת הַקֵּץ לַעֲשׂוֹת כְּמוֹ שֶׁאָמַר לְאַבְרָהָם אָבִינוּ בִּבְרִית בֵּין הַבְּתָרִים, שֶׁנֶּאֱמַר: "וַיֹּאמֶר לְאַבְרָם, יָדֹעַ תֵּדַע כִּי גֵר יִהְיֶה זַרְעֲךָ בְּאֶרֶץ לֹא לָהֶם, וַעֲבָדוּם וְעִנּוּ אֹתָם אַרְבַּע מֵאוֹת שָׁנָה. וְגַם אֶת הַגּוֹי אֲשֶׁר יַעֲבֹדוּ דָּן אָנֹכִי, וְאַחֲרֵי כֵן יֵצְאוּ בִּרְכֻשׁ גָּדוֹל."

Barukh shomeir havtachato l'Yisra'eil, barukh Hu. SheHaKadosh Barukh Hu chishav et hakeitz la'asot k'mo she'amar l'Avraham Avinu bivrit bein hab'tarim, shene'emar: "Vayomer l'Avram, yado'a teida ki geir yihye zar'akha b'eretz lo lahem, va'avadum v'inu otam arba mei'ot shana. V'gam et hagoy asher ya'avodu dan Anokhi, v'acharei khein yeitz'u birkhush gadol."

Blessed is the One who keeps His promise to Israel, blessed be He. For the Holy One calculated the end of the exile in order to fulfill what He had said to our forefather Abraham, during the Covenant between the Pieces, as it says: "He said to Abram: You should surely know that your descendants will be strangers in a land that is not theirs, and they will enslave them and afflict them four hundred years. But I will judge that nation for whom they will toil, and afterwards they will leave with great wealth."

Cover the matzah, lift your wine cup, and recite the following:

וְהִיא שֶׁעָמְדָה לַאֲבוֹתֵינוּ וְלָנוּ. שֶׁלֹּא אֶחָד בִּלְבָד עָמַד עָלֵינוּ לְכַלּוֹתֵנוּ, אֶלָּא שֶׁבְּכָל דּוֹר וָדוֹר עוֹמְדִים עָלֵינוּ לְכַלּוֹתֵנוּ, וְהַקָּדוֹשׁ בָּרוּךְ הוּא מַצִּילֵנוּ מִיָּדָם.

V'hi she'am'da la'avoteinu v'lanu. Shelo echad bilvad amad aleinu l'khaloteinu, ela sheb'khol dor vador om'dim aleinu l'khaloteinu, v'HaKadosh Barukh Hu matzileinu miyadam.

And it is this [promise] that continues to hold for our ancestors and for us, since it is not only one nation that rose up to destroy us: In every single generation they strive to destroy us, but the Holy One rescues us from their hands.

Put the cup back down, and uncover the matzah once again.

צֵא וּלְמַד מַה בִּקֵּשׁ לָבָן הָאֲרַמִּי לַעֲשׂוֹת לְיַעֲקֹב אָבִינוּ, שֶׁפַּרְעֹה לֹא גָזַר אֶלָּא עַל הַזְּכָרִים, וְלָבָן בִּקֵּשׁ לַעֲקֹר אֶת הַכֹּל. שֶׁנֶּאֱמַר: "אֲרַמִּי אֹבֵד אָבִי וַיֵּרֶד מִצְרַיְמָה, וַיָּגָר שָׁם בִּמְתֵי מְעָט, וַיְהִי שָׁם לְגוֹי גָּדוֹל עָצוּם וָרָב."

Tzei ulmad ma bikeish Lavan ha'Arami la'asot l'Ya'akov Avinu, shePar'o lo gazar ela al haz'kharim, v'Lavan bikeish la'akor et hakol. Shene'emar: "Arami oveid avi vayeired Mitzrayma, vayagor sham bimtei m'at vayhi sham l'goy gadol atzum varav."

Go learn what Laban the Aramean sought to do to our forefather Jacob, for Pharaoh only decreed death to the males but Laban sought to eliminate the whole nation. As it says: "An Aramean oppressed my forefather and he went down to Egypt. He dwelled there with few people and there became a great, powerful, and numerous nation."

וַיֵּרֶד מִצְרַיְמָה—אָנוּס עַל פִּי הַדִּבּוּר. וַיָּגָר שָׁם—מְלַמֵּד שֶׁלֹּא יָרַד יַעֲקֹב אָבִינוּ לְהִשְׁתַּקֵּעַ בְּמִצְרַיִם אֶלָּא לָגוּר שָׁם, שֶׁנֶּאֱמַר: "וַיֹּאמְרוּ אֶל פַּרְעֹה, לָגוּר בָּאָרֶץ בָּאנוּ, כִּי אֵין מִרְעֶה לַצֹּאן אֲשֶׁר לַעֲבָדֶיךָ, כִּי כָבֵד הָרָעָב בְּאֶרֶץ כְּנָעַן, וְעַתָּה יֵשְׁבוּ נָא עֲבָדֶיךָ בְּאֶרֶץ גֹּשֶׁן.‏"

Vayeired Mitzrayma—anu al pi hadibur. Vayagor sham—m'lameid shelo yarad Ya'akov Avinu l'hishtake'a b'Mitzrayim ela lagur sham, shene'emar: "Vayom'ru el Par'o, lagur ba'aretz banu, ki ein mir'e latzon asher la'avadekha, ki khaveid hara'av b'eretz K'na'an, v'ata yeish'vu na avadekha b'eretz Goshen."

"And he went down to Egypt"—compelled by the Divine word. "He dwelled there"—this teaches that our forefather Jacob didn't go down to settle in Egypt but to sojourn there, as it says: "They said to Pharaoh: We have come to sojourn in the land, since there is not enough pasture for your servants' flocks, the famine being severe in the land of Canaan. Please let your servants stay in the land of Goshen."

בִּמְתֵי מְעָט—כְּמָה שֶׁנֶּאֱמַר: "בְּשִׁבְעִים נֶפֶשׁ יָרְדוּ אֲבֹתֶיךָ מִצְרַיְמָה, וְעַתָּה שָׂמְךָ יְהֹוָה אֱלֹהֶיךָ כְּכוֹכְבֵי הַשָּׁמַיִם לָרֹב.‏"

Bimtei m'at—k'ma shene'emar: "B'shiv'im nefesh yar'du avotekha Mitzrayma, v'ata sam'kha Adonai Elohekha k'khokh'vei hashamayim larov."

"With few people"—as it says: "Your ancestors came down to Egypt with seventy people, and now *HaShem*, your God, has made you as numerous as the stars of the sky."

וַיְהִי שָׁם לְגוֹי—מְלַמֵּד שֶׁהָיוּ יִשְׂרָאֵל מְצֻיָּנִים שָׁם.

Vayhi sham l'goy—m'lameid shehayu Yisra'eil m'tzuyanim sham.

"And there became a nation"—this teaches that Israel stood out there.

גָּדוֹל עָצוּם—כְּמָה שֶׁנֶּאֱמַר: "וּבְנֵי יִשְׂרָאֵל פָּרוּ וַיִּשְׁרְצוּ וַיִּרְבּוּ וַיַּעַצְמוּ בִּמְאֹד מְאֹד, וַתִּמָּלֵא הָאָרֶץ אֹתָם.

Gadol atzum—k'ma shene'emar: "Uvnei Yisra'eil paru vayishr'tzu vayirbu vaya'atzmu bim'od m'od, vatimalei ha'aretz otam."

"Great, powerful"—as it is says: "And the children of Israel multiplied and swarmed and grew exceedingly numerous and strong, and the land became filled with them."

וָרָב—כְּמָה שֶׁנֶּאֱמַר: "רְבָבָה כְּצֶמַח הַשָּׂדֶה נְתַתִּיךְ, וַתִּרְבִּי וַתִּגְדְּלִי וַתָּבֹאִי בַּעֲדִי עֲדָיִים, שָׁדַיִם נָכֹנוּ וּשְׂעָרֵךְ צִמֵּחַ, וְאַתְּ עֵרֹם וְעֶרְיָה. וָאֶעֱבֹר עָלַיִךְ וָאֶרְאֵךְ מִתְבּוֹסֶסֶת בְּדָמָיִךְ, וָאֹמַר לָךְ בְּדָמַיִךְ חֲיִי, וָאֹמַר לָךְ בְּדָמַיִךְ חֲיִי."

Varav—k'ma shene'emar: "R'vava k'tzemach hasade n'tatikh, vatirbi vatigd'li vatavo'i ba'adi adayim, shadayim nakhonu us'areikh tzime'ach, v'at eirom v'erya. Va'e'evor alayikh va'ereikh mitboseset b'damayikh, va'omar lakh b'damayikh chayi, va'omar lakh b'damayikh chayi."

"And numerous"—as it says: "I let you grow as numerous as the plants of the field, and you developed more until you became beautiful—your breasts set and your hair sprouted, but you were naked and barren. I passed by you and I saw you wallowing in your blood, and I said to you, 'By your blood shall you live'; I said to you, 'By your blood shall you live.'"

"וַיָּרֵעוּ אֹתָנוּ הַמִּצְרִים וַיְעַנּוּנוּ, וַיִּתְּנוּ עָלֵינוּ עֲבֹדָה קָשָׁה."

"Vayarei'u otanu haMitzrim vay'anunu, vayit'nu aleinu avoda kasha."

"The Egyptians were evil to us, oppressed us, and imposed hard labor upon us."

וַיָּרֵעוּ אֹתָנוּ הַמִּצְרִים—כְּמָה שֶׁנֶּאֱמַר: "הָבָה נִתְחַכְּמָה לוֹ פֶּן יִרְבֶּה, וְהָיָה כִּי תִקְרֶאנָה מִלְחָמָה וְנוֹסַף גַּם הוּא עַל שֹׂנְאֵינוּ, וְנִלְחַם בָּנוּ וְעָלָה מִן הָאָרֶץ."

Vayarei'u otanu haMitzrim—k'ma shene'emar: "Hava nitchak'ma lo pen yirbe, v'haya ki tikrena milchama v'nosaf gam hu al son'einu, v'nilcham banu v'ala min ha'aretz."

"The Egyptians were evil to us"—as it says: "Let us deal shrewdly with them, otherwise they will multiply and in the event of war they will join our enemies, fighting against us and rising up from the land."

וַיְעַנּוּנוּ—כְּמָה שֶׁנֶּאֱמַר: "וַיָּשִׂימוּ עָלָיו
שָׂרֵי מִסִּים לְמַעַן עַנֹּתוֹ בְּסִבְלֹתָם, וַיִּבֶן עָרֵי
מִסְכְּנוֹת לְפַרְעֹה, אֶת פִּתֹם וְאֶת רַעַמְסֵס."

Vay'anunu—k'ma shene'emar: "Vayasimu alav sarei misim l'ma'an anoto b'sivlotam, vayiven arei misk'not l'Far'o, et Pitom v'et Ra'amses."

"Oppressed us"—as it says: "They placed taskmasters over them in order to oppress them with their burdens, and they built the storage cities of Pitom and Ra'amses."

וַיִּתְּנוּ עָלֵינוּ עֲבֹדָה קָשָׁה—כְּמָה שֶׁנֶּאֱמַר:
"וַיַּעֲבִדוּ מִצְרַיִם אֶת בְּנֵי יִשְׂרָאֵל בְּפָרֶךְ."

Vayit'nu aleinu avoda kasha—k'ma shene'emar: "Vaya'avidu Mitzrayim et B'nei Yisra'eil b'farekh."

"And imposed hard labor upon us"—as it says: "And they enslaved the Children of Israel with backbreaking work."

"וַנִּצְעַק אֶל יְהֹוָה אֱלֹהֵי אֲבֹתֵינוּ, וַיִּשְׁמַע יְהֹוָה
אֶת קֹלֵנוּ, וַיַּרְא אֶת עָנְיֵנוּ וְאֶת עֲמָלֵנוּ וְאֶת
לַחֲצֵנוּ."

"Vanitz'ak el Adonai Elohei avoteinu, vayishma Adonai et koleinu, vayar et onyeinu v'et amaleinu v'et lachatzeinu."

"We cried out to HaShem, the God of our forefathers, and HaShem heard our voice and saw our affliction, our toil, our oppression."

וַנִּצְעַק אֶל יְהֹוָה אֱלֹהֵי אֲבֹתֵינוּ—כְּמָה
שֶׁנֶּאֱמַר: "וַיְהִי בַיָּמִים הָרַבִּים הָהֵם וַיָּמָת
מֶלֶךְ מִצְרַיִם, וַיֵּאָנְחוּ בְנֵי יִשְׂרָאֵל מִן הָעֲבֹדָה
וַיִּזְעָקוּ, וַתַּעַל שַׁוְעָתָם אֶל הָאֱלֹהִים מִן
הָעֲבֹדָה."

Vanitz'ak el Adonai Elohei avoteinu—k'ma shene'emar: "Vayhi vayamim harabim haheim vayamot melekh Mitzrayim, vayei'an'chu V'nei Yisra'eil min ha'avoda vayiz'aku, vata'al shav'atam el ha'Elohim min ha'avoda."

"We cried out to HaShem, the God of our forefathers"—as it says: "During that long period the king of Egypt died, and the Children of Israel groaned under their bondage and cried out, and their cry from bondage ascended to God."

וַיִּשְׁמַע יְהֹוָה אֶת קֹלֵנוּ—כְּמָה שֶׁנֶּאֱמַר:
"וַיִּשְׁמַע אֱלֹהִים אֶת נַאֲקָתָם, וַיִּזְכֹּר אֱלֹהִים
אֶת בְּרִיתוֹ אֶת אַבְרָהָם אֶת יִצְחָק וְאֶת
יַעֲקֹב."

Vayishma Adonai et koleinu—k'ma shene'emar: "Vayishma Elohim et na'akatam, vayizkor Elohim et b'rito et Avraham et Yitzchak v'et Ya'akov."

"And *HaShem* heard our voice"—as it says: "God heard their cries, and God remembered His covenant with Abraham and with Isaac and with Jacob."

וַיַּרְא אֶת עָנְיֵנוּ—זוֹ פְּרִישׁוּת דֶּרֶךְ אֶרֶץ, כְּמָה שֶׁנֶּאֱמַר: "וַיַּרְא אֱלֹהִים אֶת בְּנֵי יִשְׂרָאֵל וַיֵּדַע אֱלֹהִים."

Vayar et onyeinu—zo p'rishut derekh eretz, k'ma shene'emar: "Vayar Elohim et B'nei Yisra'eil vayeida Elohim."

"And saw our affliction"—this refers to conjugal separation, as it says: "God saw the Children of Israel, and God knew."

וְאֶת עֲמָלֵנוּ—אֵלּוּ הַבָּנִים, כְּמָה שֶׁנֶּאֱמַר: "כָּל הַבֵּן הַיִּלּוֹד הַיְאֹרָה תַּשְׁלִיכֻהוּ וְכָל הַבַּת תְּחַיּוּן."

V'et amaleinu—eilu habanim k'ma shene'emar: "Kol habein hayilod haY'ora tashlikhuhu v'khol habat t'chayun."

"Our toil"—this refers to the sons, as it says: "Throw every boy that is born into the Nile, and let every girl live."

The Conflicting Truths of Passover

For an African American Jew, Passover is bound up in both the collective spiritual and religious moment of national emancipation and freedom, and the social reality that, as James Baldwin wrote, "the Jewish travail occurred across the sea and America rescued him from the house of bondage. But America is the house of bondage for the Negro, and no country can rescue him."

These two conflicting truths make it difficult to reconcile the divide of communal celebration with the greater American Jewish whole, and the despair when that selfsame community refuses to acknowledge the vast difference of circumstance of a legacy not even two centuries abolished—or even fully extinct. And to that resistance against our voices and experiences being heard, African American Jews—and Jews of color as a whole—are robustly declaring, "Dayenu!"

— *"MaNishtana" (Shais Rishon)*

וְאֶת לַחֲצֵנוּ—זֶה הַדְּחַק, כְּמָה שֶׁנֶּאֱמַר: "וְגַם רָאִיתִי אֶת הַלַּחַץ אֲשֶׁר מִצְרַיִם לֹחֲצִים אֹתָם."

V'et lachatzeinu—ze had'chak, k'ma shene'emar: "V'gam ra'iti et halachatz asher Mitzrayim lochatzim otam."

"Our oppression"—this refers to the pressure, as it says: "And I also have seen the oppression with which the Egyptians oppress them."

"וַיּוֹצִאֵנוּ יְהוָה מִמִּצְרַיִם בְּיָד חֲזָקָה וּבִזְרֹעַ נְטוּיָה וּבְמֹרָא גָּדֹל וּבְאֹתוֹת וּבְמֹפְתִים."

"Vayotzi'einu Adonai miMitzrayim b'yad chazaka uvizro'a n'tuya uvmora gadol uv'otot uvmof'tim."

"HaShem took us out of Egypt with a mighty hand and an outstretched arm, with great awe, with signs and wonders."

וַיּוֹצִאֵנוּ יְהוָה מִמִּצְרַיִם—לֹא עַל־יְדֵי מַלְאָךְ, וְלֹא עַל־יְדֵי שָׂרָף, וְלֹא עַל־יְדֵי שָׁלִיחַ, אֶלָּא הַקָּדוֹשׁ בָּרוּךְ הוּא בִּכְבוֹדוֹ וּבְעַצְמוֹ, שֶׁנֶּאֱמַר: "וְעָבַרְתִּי בְאֶרֶץ מִצְרַיִם בַּלַּיְלָה הַזֶּה, וְהִכֵּיתִי כָל בְּכוֹר בְּאֶרֶץ מִצְרַיִם מֵאָדָם וְעַד בְּהֵמָה, וּבְכָל אֱלֹהֵי מִצְרַיִם אֶעֱשֶׂה שְׁפָטִים, אֲנִי יְהוָה."

Vayotzi'einu Adonai miMitzrayim—lo al y'dei mal'akh, v'lo al y'dei saraf, v'lo al y'dei shali'ach, ela HaKadosh Barukh Hu bikhvodo uv'atzmo, shene'emar: "V'avarti v'eretz Mitzrayim balaila haze, v'hikeiti khol b'khor b'eretz Mitzrayim mei'adam v'ad b'heima, uvkhol elohei Mitzrayim e'ese sh'fatim, ani Adonai."

"HaShem took us out of Egypt"—not through an angel, nor through a seraph, nor through a messenger, but the Holy One Himself, as it says: "On that night, I will pass through the land of Egypt and I will strike down every firstborn in the land of Egypt, from man to beast, and I will mete out punishments to all of Egypt's gods—I am HaShem."

וְעָבַרְתִּי בְאֶרֶץ מִצְרַיִם בַּלַּיְלָה הַזֶּה— אֲנִי וְלֹא מַלְאָךְ. וְהִכֵּיתִי כָל בְּכוֹר בְּאֶרֶץ מִצְרַיִם—אֲנִי וְלֹא שָׂרָף. וּבְכָל אֱלֹהֵי מִצְרַיִם אֶעֱשֶׂה שְׁפָטִים—אֲנִי וְלֹא הַשָּׁלִיחַ. אֲנִי יְהוָה—אֲנִי הוּא וְלֹא אַחֵר.

V'avarti v'eretz Mitzrayim balaila haze—ani v'lo mal'akh. V'hikeiti khol b'khor b'eretz Mitzrayim—ani v'lo saraf. Uvkhol elohei Mitzrayim e'ese sh'fatim—ani v'lo hashali'ach. Ani Adonai—ani hu v'lo acheir.

"On that night, I will pass through the land of Egypt"—I and not an angel. "And I will strike down every firstborn"—I and not a seraph. "And I will mete out punishments to all of Egypt's gods"—I and not a messenger. "I am HaShem"—it is I and no one else.

בְּיָד חֲזָקָה—זוֹ הַדֶּבֶר, כְּמָה שֶׁנֶּאֱמַר: "הִנֵּה יַד יְהוָה הוֹיָה בְּמִקְנְךָ אֲשֶׁר בַּשָּׂדֶה, בַּסּוּסִים, בַּחֲמֹרִים, בַּגְּמַלִּים, בַּבָּקָר וּבַצֹּאן, דֶּבֶר כָּבֵד מְאֹד."

B'yad chazaka—zo hadever, k'ma shene'emar: "Hinei yad Adonai hoya b'mikn'kha asher basade, basusim, bachamorim, bag'malim, babakar uvatzon, dever kaveid m'od."

"With a mighty hand"—this refers to the pestilence, as it says: "Look! *HaShem*'s hand is upon your livestock in the field: the horses, donkeys, camels, cattle, and flocks. It is a very severe pestilence."

וּבִזְרֹעַ נְטוּיָה—זוֹ הַחֶרֶב, כְּמָה שֶׁנֶּאֱמַר: "וְחַרְבּוֹ שְׁלוּפָה בְּיָדוֹ, נְטוּיָה עַל יְרוּשָׁלַיִם."

Uvizro'a n'tuya—zo hacherev, k'ma shene'emar: "V'charbo sh'lufa b'yado, n'tuya al Y'rushalayim."

"And an outstretched arm"—this refers to the sword, as it is written: "His sword drawn in his hand, stretched out over Jerusalem."

וּבְמֹרָא גָּדֹל—זוֹ גִּלּוּי שְׁכִינָה, כְּמָה שֶׁנֶּאֱמַר: "אוֹ הֲנִסָּה אֱלֹהִים לָבוֹא לָקַחַת לוֹ גוֹי מִקֶּרֶב גּוֹי בְּמַסֹּת בְּאֹתֹת וּבְמוֹפְתִים וּבְמִלְחָמָה וּבְיָד חֲזָקָה וּבִזְרוֹעַ נְטוּיָה וּבְמוֹרָאִים גְּדֹלִים, כְּכֹל אֲשֶׁר עָשָׂה לָכֶם יְהוָה אֱלֹהֵיכֶם בְּמִצְרַיִם לְעֵינֶיךָ."

Uvmora gadol—zo gilu'i Sh'khina, k'ma shene'emar: "O hanisa Elohim lavo lakachat lo goy mikerev goy b'masot b'otot uvmof'tim uvmilchama uvyad chazaka uvizro'a uvnetuya uvmora'im g'dolim, k'khol asher asa lakhem Adonai Eloheikhem b'Mitzrayim l'einekha."

"With great awe"—this refers to the revelation of the Divine Presence, as it says: "Has any god ventured to go and take for himself one nation from the midst of another through trials, signs, and wonders, through war, with a mighty hand and an outstretched arm, with awesome feats, like everything that *HaShem*, your God, did for you in Egypt in front of your eyes?"

וּבְאֹתוֹת—זֶה הַמַּטֶּה, כְּמָה שֶׁנֶּאֱמַר: "וְאֶת הַמַּטֶּה הַזֶּה תִּקַּח בְּיָדֶךָ אֲשֶׁר תַּעֲשֶׂה בּוֹ אֶת הָאֹתוֹת."

Uv'otot—ze hamate, k'ma shene'emar: "V'et hamate haze tikach b'yadekha asher ta'ase bo et ha'otot."

"With signs"—this refers to the staff, as it says: "Take in your hand this staff through which you will perform the signs."

וּבְמֹפְתִים—זֶה הַדָּם, כְּמָה שֶׁנֶּאֱמַר: "וְנָתַתִּי מוֹפְתִים בַּשָּׁמַיִם וּבָאָרֶץ."

Uvmof'tim—ze hadam, k'ma shene'emar: "V'natati mof'tim bashamayim uva'aretz."

"And wonders"—this refers to the blood, as it says: "And I will set my wonders in the skies and on the earth."

THE 10 PLAGUES

Read out loud the three signs of the Divine below, and after each one, dip your finger in the wine and tap it on the plate:

דָּם, וָאֵשׁ, וְתִימְרוֹת עָשָׁן.

Dam va'eish v'tim'rot ashan

"Blood and fire and pillars of smoke."

דָּבָר אַחֵר: בְּיָד חֲזָקָה — שְׁתַּיִם, וּבִזְרֹעַ נְטוּיָה — שְׁתַּיִם, וּבְמֹרָא גָּדֹל — שְׁתַּיִם, וּבְאֹתוֹת — שְׁתַּיִם, וּבְמֹפְתִים — שְׁתַּיִם.

Davar acheir: b'yad chazaka—sh'tayim, uvizro'a n'tuya—sh'tayim, uvmora gadol—sh'tayim, uv'otot—sh'tayim, uvmof'tim—sh'tayim.

Another interpretation: "With a mighty hand"—two [plagues]; "and an outstretched arm"—two; "with great awe"—two; "with signs"—two; "and wonders"—two.

The Ten Plagues

As you recite each one, dip your finger in the wine and tap it on the plate:

אֵלּוּ עֶשֶׂר מַכּוֹת שֶׁהֵבִיא הַקָּדוֹשׁ בָּרוּךְ הוּא
עַל הַמִּצְרִים בְּמִצְרַיִם, וְאֵלּוּ הֵן:

Eilu eser makot sheheivi HaKadosh Barukh Hu al haMitzrim b'Mitzrayim, v'eilu hein:

The following are the Ten Plagues that the Holy One brought on the Egyptians in Egypt:

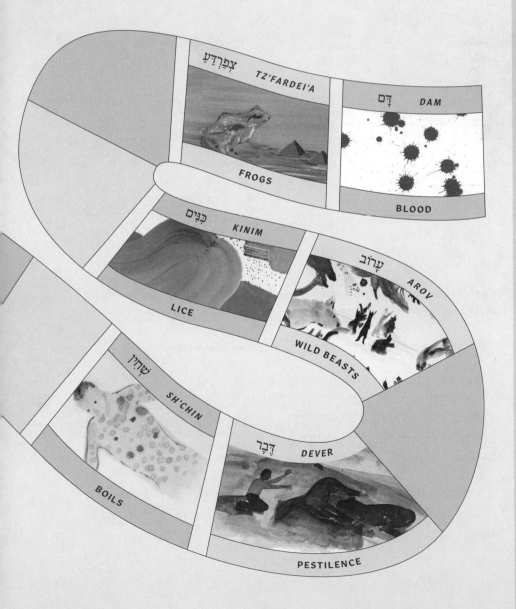

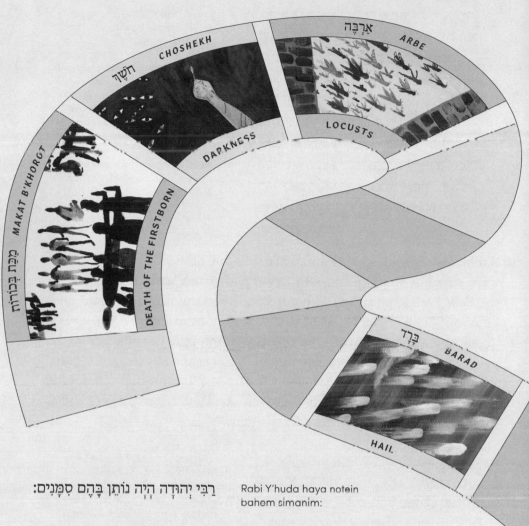

רַבִּי יְהוּדָה הָיָה נוֹתֵן בָּהֶם סִמָּנִים:

Rabi Y'huda haya notein bahem simanim:

Rabbi Yehuda made mnemonics for the plagues:

After reading each of Rabbi Yehuda's mnemonics, dip your finger in the wine and tap it on the plate:

דְּצַ"ךְ, עַדַ"שׁ, בְּאַחַ"ב.

D'tzakh, adash, b'achav

What are some things that plague us all today?

D'tzakh [the Hebrew initials of the first three plagues], *Adash* [the Hebrew initials of the second three plagues], *B'achav* [the Hebrew initials of the last four plagues].

רַבִּי יוֹסֵי הַגְּלִילִי אוֹמֵר: מִנַּיִן אַתָּה אוֹמֵר שֶׁלָּקוּ הַמִּצְרִים בְּמִצְרַיִם עֶשֶׂר מַכּוֹת וְעַל הַיָּם לָקוּ חֲמִשִּׁים מַכּוֹת? בְּמִצְרַיִם מַה הוּא אוֹמֵר: "וַיֹּאמְרוּ הַחַרְטֻמִּם אֶל פַּרְעֹה, אֶצְבַּע אֱלֹהִים הִוא." וְעַל הַיָּם מָה הוּא אוֹמֵר: "וַיַּרְא יִשְׂרָאֵל אֶת הַיָּד הַגְּדֹלָה אֲשֶׁר עָשָׂה יְהוָה בְּמִצְרַיִם, וַיִּירְאוּ הָעָם אֶת יְהוָה וַיַּאֲמִינוּ בַּיהוָה וּבְמֹשֶׁה עַבְדּוֹ." כַּמָּה לָקוּ בְּאֶצְבַּע? עֶשֶׂר מַכּוֹת. אֱמוֹר מֵעַתָּה, בְּמִצְרַיִם לָקוּ עֶשֶׂר מַכּוֹת וְעַל הַיָּם לָקוּ חֲמִשִּׁים מַכּוֹת.

Rabi Yosei HaG'lili omeir: Minayin ata omeir shelaku haMitzrim b'Mitzrayim eser makot v'al hayam laku chamishim makot? B'Mitzrayim ma hu omeir: "Vayom'ru hachartumim el Par'o, etzba Elohim hi." V'al hayam ma hu omeir: "Vayar Yisra'eil et hayad hag'dola asher asa Adonai b'Mitzrayim, vayir'u ha'am et Adonai vaya'aminu bAdonai uvMoshe avdo." Kama laku b'etzba? Eser makot. Emor mei'ata b'Mitzrayim laku eser makot v'al hayam laku chamishim makot.

Rabbi Yosi Hagelili says: "From where can you derive that the Egyptians were struck with ten plagues in Egypt and struck with fifty plagues at the Sea? Well, concerning Egypt it says 'Then the magicians said unto Pharaoh: "This is the *finger* of God," ' and concerning the Sea it says, 'Israel saw *HaShem*'s great *hand* that he set upon the Egyptians, and the people feared *HaShem*; they believed in *HaShem* and His servant Moses.' With how many were they struck by the finger? Ten plagues. Therefore, you can conclude that in Egypt they were struck with ten plagues and at the Sea they were struck with fifty plagues."

רַבִּי אֱלִיעֶזֶר אוֹמֵר: מִנַּיִן שֶׁכָּל מַכָּה וּמַכָּה שֶׁהֵבִיא הַקָּדוֹשׁ בָּרוּךְ הוּא עַל הַמִּצְרִים בְּמִצְרַיִם הָיְתָה שֶׁל אַרְבַּע מַכּוֹת? שֶׁנֶּאֱמַר: "יְשַׁלַּח בָּם חֲרוֹן אַפּוֹ, עֶבְרָה, וָזַעַם, וְצָרָה, מִשְׁלַחַת מַלְאֲכֵי רָעִים." עֶבְרָה—אַחַת, וָזַעַם—שְׁתַּיִם, וְצָרָה—שָׁלֹשׁ, מִשְׁלַחַת מַלְאֲכֵי רָעִים—אַרְבַּע. אֱמוֹר מֵעַתָּה, בְּמִצְרַיִם לָקוּ אַרְבָּעִים מַכּוֹת וְעַל הַיָּם לָקוּ מָאתַיִם מַכּוֹת.

Rabi Eli'ezer omeir: Minayin shekol maka umaka sheheivi HaKadosh Barukh Hu al haMitzrim b'Mitzrayim hay'ta shel arba makot? Shene'emar: "Y'shalach bam charon apo, evra, vaza'am, v'tzara, mishlachat mal'akhei ra'im." Evra—achat, vaza'am—sh'tayim, v'tzara—shalosh, mishlachat mal'akhei ra'im—arba. Emor mei'ata, b'Mitzrayim laku arba'im makot v'al hayam laku matayim makot.

Rabbi Eliezer says: "From where can you derive that every plague that the Holy One brought upon the Egyptians in Egypt consisted of four plagues? As it says: 'He sent upon them His fierce anger, wrath, fury, trouble, a band of baneful messengers.' 'Wrath'—one; 'fury'—two; 'trouble'—three; 'a band of baneful messengers'—four. Therefore, you can conclude that in Egypt they were struck with forty plagues and at the Sea they were struck with two hundred plagues."

רַבִּי עֲקִיבָא אוֹמֵר: מִנַּיִן שֶׁכָּל מַכָּה וּמַכָּה שֶׁהֵבִיא הַקָּדוֹשׁ בָּרוּךְ הוּא עַל הַמִּצְרִים בְּמִצְרַיִם הָיְתָה שֶׁל חָמֵשׁ מַכּוֹת? שֶׁנֶּאֱמַר: "יְשַׁלַּח בָּם חֲרוֹן אַפּוֹ, עֶבְרָה, וָזַעַם, וְצָרָה, מִשְׁלַחַת מַלְאֲכֵי רָעִים." חֲרוֹן אַפּוֹ—אַחַת, עֶבְרָה—שְׁתַּיִם, וָזַעַם—שָׁלוֹשׁ, וְצָרָה—אַרְבַּע, מִשְׁלַחַת מַלְאֲכֵי רָעִים—חָמֵשׁ. אֱמוֹר מֵעַתָּה, בְּמִצְרַיִם לָקוּ חֲמִשִּׁים מַכּוֹת וְעַל הַיָּם לָקוּ חֲמִשִּׁים וּמָאתִים מַכּוֹת.

Rabi Akiva omeir: Minayin shekol maka umaka sheheivi HaKadosh Barukh Hu al haMitzrim b'Mitzrayim hay'ta shel chameish makot? Shene'emar: "Y'shalach bam charon apo, evra, vaza'am, v'tzara, mishlachat mal'akhei ra'im." Charon apo—achat, evra—sh'tayim, vaza'am—shalosh, v'tzara—arba, mishlachat mal'akhei ra'im—chameish. Emor mei'ata, b'Mitzrayim laku chamishim makot v'al hayam laku chamishim umatayim makot.

Rabbi Akiva says: "From where can you derive that every plague that the Holy One brought upon the Egyptians in Egypt consisted of five plagues? As it says: 'He sent upon them His fierce anger, wrath, fury, trouble, a band of baneful messengers.' 'His fierce anger'—one; 'wrath'—two; 'fury'—three; 'trouble'—four; 'a band of baneful messengers'—five. Therefore, you can conclude that in Egypt they were struck with fifty plagues and at the Sea they were struck with two hundred and fifty plagues."

Dayenu

It would've been enough: Is there a more profound expression of gratitude? This part of the Haggadah is literally us counting our blessings, which, if done sparingly, is a wonderful thing to do.

    During this song, Persian Jews whack each other with scallions to symbolize the whips from our Egyptian overlords. (Do this sparingly too.)

כַּמָּה מַעֲלוֹת טוֹבוֹת לַמָּקוֹם עָלֵינוּ!

1   אִלּוּ הוֹצִיאָנוּ מִמִּצְרַיִם, וְלֹא עָשָׂה בָהֶם שְׁפָטִים, דַּיֵּנוּ.

2   אִלּוּ עָשָׂה בָהֶם שְׁפָטִים, וְלֹא עָשָׂה בֵאלֹהֵיהֶם, דַּיֵּנוּ.

3   אִלּוּ עָשָׂה בֵאלֹהֵיהֶם, וְלֹא הָרַג אֶת בְּכוֹרֵיהֶם, דַּיֵּנוּ.

4   אִלּוּ הָרַג אֶת בְּכוֹרֵיהֶם, וְלֹא נָתַן לָנוּ אֶת מָמוֹנָם, דַּיֵּנוּ.

5   אִלּוּ נָתַן לָנוּ אֶת מָמוֹנָם, וְלֹא קָרַע לָנוּ אֶת הַיָּם, דַּיֵּנוּ.

6   אִלּוּ קָרַע לָנוּ אֶת הַיָּם, וְלֹא הֶעֱבִירָנוּ בְּתוֹכוֹ בֶּחָרָבָה, דַּיֵּנוּ.

7   אִלּוּ הֶעֱבִירָנוּ בְּתוֹכוֹ בֶּחָרָבָה, וְלֹא שִׁקַּע צָרֵנוּ בְּתוֹכוֹ, דַּיֵּנוּ.

8   אִלּוּ שִׁקַּע צָרֵנוּ בְּתוֹכוֹ, וְלֹא סִפֵּק צָרְכֵּנוּ בַּמִּדְבָּר אַרְבָּעִים שָׁנָה, דַּיֵּנוּ.

9   אִלּוּ סִפֵּק צָרְכֵּנוּ בַּמִּדְבָּר אַרְבָּעִים שָׁנָה, וְלֹא הֶאֱכִילָנוּ אֶת הַמָּן, דַּיֵּנוּ.

How many good things did
God bestow upon us!

1 If He had taken us out of Egypt but
   not meted out punishments against
   them, it would have been enough.

2 If He had meted out punishments
   against them but not done so against
   their gods, it would have been enough.

3 If He had done so against their gods
   but not killed their firstborn, it would
   have been enough.

4 If He had killed their firstborn but not
   given us their wealth, it would have
   been enough.

5 If He had given us their wealth but not
   split the sea for us, it would have been
   enough.

6 If He had split the sea for us but not
   taken us through it on dry land, it
   would have been enough.

7 If He had taken us through it on dry
   land but not drowned our enemies in
   it, it would have been enough.

8 If He had drowned our enemies in it
   but not provided for our needs in the
   wilderness for forty years, it would
   have been enough.

9 If He had provided for our needs in
   the wilderness for forty years but not
   fed us the manna, it would have been
   enough.

Kama ma'alot tovot laMakom aleinu

1 Ilu hotzi'anu
   miMitzrayim,
   v'lo asa vahem
   sh'fatim, dayenu

2 Ilu asa vahem
   sh'fatim, v'lo
   asa veiloheihem,
   dayenu

3 Ilu asa veiloheihem,
   v'lo harag et
   b'khoreihm, dayenu

4 Ilu harag et
   b'khoreihm, v'lo natan
   lanu et mamonam,
   dayenu

5 Ilu natan lanu et
   mamonam, v'lo kara lanu
   et hayam, dayenu

6 Ilu kara lanu et hayam,
   v'lo he'eviranu b'tokho
   becharava, dayenu

7 Ilu he'eviranu b'tokho
   becharava, v'lo shika
   tzareinu b'tokho, dayenu

8 Ilu shika tzareinu b'tokho, v'lo
   sipeik tzorkeinu bamidbar arba'im
   shana, dayenu

9 Ilu sipeik tzorkeinu bamidbar
   arba'im shana, v'lo he'ekhilanu et
   haman, dayenu

If this is feeling too repetitive, take a break with Howard Jacobson's piece on dayenu as the quintessential Jewish emotion (page 131).

10 אִלּוּ הֶאֱכִילָנוּ אֶת הַמָּן, וְלֹא נָתַן לָנוּ אֶת הַשַּׁבָּת, דַּיֵּנוּ.

11 אִלּוּ נָתַן לָנוּ אֶת הַשַּׁבָּת, וְלֹא קֵרְבָנוּ לִפְנֵי הַר סִינַי, דַּיֵּנוּ.

12 אִלּוּ קֵרְבָנוּ לִפְנֵי הַר סִינַי, וְלֹא נָתַן לָנוּ אֶת הַתּוֹרָה, דַּיֵּנוּ.

13 אִלּוּ נָתַן לָנוּ אֶת הַתּוֹרָה, וְלֹא הִכְנִיסָנוּ לְאֶרֶץ יִשְׂרָאֵל, דַּיֵּנוּ.

14 אִלּוּ הִכְנִיסָנוּ לְאֶרֶץ יִשְׂרָאֵל, וְלֹא בָנָה לָנוּ אֶת בֵּית הַבְּחִירָה, דַּיֵּנוּ.

עַל אַחַת כַּמָּה וְכַמָּה טוֹבָה כְפוּלָה וּמְכֻפֶּלֶת לַמָּקוֹם עָלֵינוּ: שֶׁהוֹצִיאָנוּ מִמִּצְרַיִם, וְעָשָׂה בָהֶם שְׁפָטִים, וְעָשָׂה בֵאלֹהֵיהֶם, וְהָרַג אֶת בְּכוֹרֵיהֶם, וְנָתַן לָנוּ אֶת מָמוֹנָם, וְקָרַע לָנוּ אֶת הַיָּם, וְהֶעֱבִירָנוּ בְּתוֹכוֹ בֶּחָרָבָה, וְשִׁקַּע צָרֵנוּ בְּתוֹכוֹ, וְסִפֵּק צָרְכֵּנוּ בַּמִּדְבָּר אַרְבָּעִים שָׁנָה, וְהֶאֱכִילָנוּ אֶת הַמָּן, וְנָתַן לָנוּ אֶת הַשַּׁבָּת, וְקֵרְבָנוּ לִפְנֵי הַר סִינַי, וְנָתַן לָנוּ אֶת הַתּוֹרָה, וְהִכְנִיסָנוּ לְאֶרֶץ יִשְׂרָאֵל, וּבָנָה לָנוּ אֶת בֵּית הַבְּחִירָה לְכַפֵּר עַל כָּל עֲוֹנוֹתֵינוּ.

10 If He had fed us the manna but not given us Shabbat, it would have been enough.

11 If He had given us Shabbat but not brought us before Mount Sinai, it would have been enough.

12 If He had brought us before Mount Sinai but not given us the Torah, it would have been enough.

13 If He had given us the Torah but not brought us into the Land of Israel, it would have been enough.

14 If He had brought us into the Land of Israel but not built us the Temple, it would have been enough.

How much more so, then, should we be manifoldly grateful to God: For He took us out of Egypt, and meted out punishments against them, and did so against their gods, and killed their firstborn, and gave us their wealth, and split the sea for us, and took us through it on dry land, and drowned our enemies in it, and provided for our needs in the wilderness for forty years, and fed us the manna, and gave us Shabbat, and brought us before Mount Sinai, and gave us the Torah, and brought us into the Land of Israel, and built us the Temple to atone for all of our sins.

10 Ilu he'ekhilanu et haman, v'lo natan lanu et haShabbat, dayenu

11 Ilu natan lanu et haShabbat, v'lo keir'vanu lifnei Har Sinai, dayenu

12 Ilu keir'vanu lifnei Har Sinai, v'lo natan lanu et haTora, dayenu

13 Ilu natan lanu et haTora, v'lo hikhnisanu l'Eretz Yisra'eil, dayenu

14 Ilu hikhnisanu l'Eretz Yisra'eil, v'lo vana lanu et Beit HaB'chira, dayenu

Al achat kama v'khama tova k'fula umkhupelet laMakom aleinu: shehotzi'anu miMitzrayim, v'asa vahem sh'fatim, v'asa veiloheihem, v'harag et b'khoreihm, v'natan lanu et mamonam, v'kara lanu et hayam, v'he'eviranu b'tokho becharava, v'shika tzareinu b'tokho, v'sipeik tzorkeinu bamidbar arba'im shana, v'he'ekhilanu et haman, v'natan lanu et haShabbat, v'keir'vanu lifnei Har Sinai, v'natan lanu et haTora, v'hikhnisanu l'Eretz Yisra'eil, uvana lanu et Beit HaB'chira l'khapeir al kol avonoteinu.

My Big, Gay Seder Wedding

Three decades ago, I brought Mark to our family Seder for the first time. We'd been together the previous Passover, too, but at that point I'd been too embarrassed to bring my boyfriend to this annual gathering of family and friends. I thought my parents might be uncomfortable. I thought our guests might be uncomfortable. I thought Mark might be uncomfortable. I thought I would be uncomfortable.

The next year, I got over myself, realizing I wanted to share a tradition I love with the man I love—and I wanted to share him with our Seder guests.

Exactly twenty years later, we eloped the afternoon before the first Seder. Seated around the table that night with the people who now knew Mark as part of my family—and, by extension, theirs—we made the announcement after the Four Questions, adding: "Why is this night different from all thirty-six others? Because tonight, we are married." We held up our hands, with our new silver wedding rings.

Getting married? *Dayenu,* it would have been enough for us. Having a Seder as our wedding celebration? Even better.

—*Wayne Hoffman*

רַבָּן גַּמְלִיאֵל הָיָה אוֹמֵר: כָּל שֶׁלֹּא אָמַר שְׁלֹשָׁה דְבָרִים אֵלּוּ בַּפֶּסַח, לֹא יָצָא יְדֵי חוֹבָתוֹ, וְאֵלּוּ הֵן—פֶּסַח, מַצָּה, וּמָרוֹר.

Rabi Gamli'eil haya omeir: Kol shelo amar sh'losha d'varim eilu baPesach lo yatza y'dei chovato, v'eilu hein—Pesach, matzah, umaror.

Rabban Gamliel would say: "Anyone who has not said the following three things on Pesach has not fulfilled their obligation: the Pesach sacrifice, matzah, and *maror*."

Now explain the shank bone:

פֶּסַח שֶׁהָיוּ אֲבוֹתֵינוּ אוֹכְלִים בִּזְמַן שֶׁבֵּית הַמִּקְדָּשׁ הָיָה קַיָם, עַל שׁוּם מָה? עַל שׁוּם שֶׁפָּסַח הַקָּדוֹשׁ בָּרוּךְ הוּא עַל בָּתֵּי אֲבוֹתֵינוּ בְּמִצְרַיִם, שֶׁנֶּאֱמַר: "וַאֲמַרְתֶּם זֶבַח פֶּסַח הוּא לַיהוָה, אֲשֶׁר פָּסַח עַל בָּתֵּי בְנֵי יִשְׂרָאֵל בְּמִצְרַיִם בְּנָגְפּוֹ אֶת מִצְרַיִם, וְאֶת בָּתֵּינוּ הִצִּיל, וַיִּקֹּד הָעָם וַיִּשְׁתַּחֲווּ."

Pesach shehayu avoteinu okh'lim bizman sheBeit HaMikdash haya kayam, al shum ma? Al shum shepasach HaKadosh Barukh Hu al batei avoteinu b'Mitzrayim, shene'emar: "Va'amartem zevach Pesach hu lAdonai, asher pasach al batei V'nei Yisra'eil b'Mitzrayim b'nogpo et Mitzrayim, v'et bateinu hitzil, vayikod ha'am vayishtachavu."

Why did our ancestors eat the Pesach sacrifice when the Temple was still standing? Because the Holy One passed over (*pasach*) the homes of our ancestors in Egypt, as it says: "You shall say: It is the passover sacrifice to the Lord, who passed over (*pasach*) the homes of the Children of Israel in Egypt when He struck down the Egyptians and saved our households. And the people bowed and prostrated themselves."

Point to or lift a matzah, then say:

מַצָּה זוֹ שֶׁאָנוּ אוֹכְלִים, עַל שׁוּם מָה? עַל שׁוּם שֶׁלֹּא הִסְפִּיק בְּצֵקָם שֶׁל אֲבוֹתֵינוּ לְהַחֲמִיץ עַד שֶׁנִּגְלָה עֲלֵיהֶם מֶלֶךְ מַלְכֵי הַמְּלָכִים הַקָּדוֹשׁ בָּרוּךְ הוּא וּגְאָלָם, שֶׁנֶּאֱמַר: "וַיֹּאפוּ אֶת הַבָּצֵק אֲשֶׁר הוֹצִיאוּ מִמִּצְרַיִם עֻגֹת מַצּוֹת, כִּי לֹא חָמֵץ, כִּי גֹרְשׁוּ מִמִּצְרַיִם וְלֹא יָכְלוּ לְהִתְמַהְמֵהַּ, וְגַם צֵדָה לֹא עָשׂוּ לָהֶם."

Matzah zo she'anu okh'lim, al shum ma? Al shum shelo hispik b'tzeikam shel avoteinu l'hachamitz ad shenigla aleihem Melekh Malkhei HaM'lakhim HaKadosh Barukh Hu ug'alam, shene'emar: "Vayofu et habatzeik asher hotzi'u miMitzrayim ugot matzahs, ki lo chameitz, ki gor'shu miMitzrayim v'lo yakh'lu l'hitmahmei'ah, v'gam tzeida lo asu lahem."

Why are we eating this matzah? Because our ancestors' dough was unable to rise before the King of kings, the Holy One, revealed Himself and redeemed them, as it says: "They baked the dough that they had brought out of Egypt into cakes of matzah, for it was not leavened, since they had been driven out of Egypt and could not delay, and they had not made provisions for themselves."

*Point to the **maror**, or bitter herbs, then say:*

מָרוֹר זֶה שֶׁאָנוּ אוֹכְלִים, עַל שׁוּם מָה? עַל שׁוּם שֶׁמֵּרְרוּ הַמִּצְרִים אֶת חַיֵּי אֲבוֹתֵינוּ בְּמִצְרַיִם, שֶׁנֶּאֱמַר: "וַיְמָרְרוּ אֶת חַיֵּיהֶם בַּעֲבֹדָה קָשָׁה בְּחֹמֶר וּבִלְבֵנִים וּבְכָל עֲבֹדָה בַּשָּׂדֶה, אֵת כָּל עֲבֹדָתָם אֲשֶׁר עָבְדוּ בָהֶם בְּפָרֶךְ."

Maror ze she'anu okh'lim, al shum mah? Al shum shemeir'ru haMitzrim et chayei avoteinu b'Mitzrayim, shene'emar: "Vaymar'ru et chayeihem ba'avoda kasha b'chomer uvilveinim uvkhol avoda basade, et kol avodatam asher av'du vahem b'farekh."

Why are we eating this *maror*? Because the Egyptians embittered (*meir'ru*) the lives of our ancestors in Egypt, as it says: "They embittered (*Vaymar'ru*) their lives with hard labor, with mortar and bricks and every type of labor in the field; every labor they forced them to do was backbreaking."

בְּכָל דּוֹר וָדוֹר חַיָּב אָדָם לִרְאוֹת אֶת עַצְמוֹ כְּאִלּוּ הוּא יָצָא מִמִּצְרַיִם, שֶׁנֶּאֱמַר: "וְהִגַּדְתָּ לְבִנְךָ בַּיּוֹם הַהוּא לֵאמֹר, בַּעֲבוּר זֶה עָשָׂה יְהֹוָה לִי בְּצֵאתִי מִמִּצְרָיִם." לֹא אֶת אֲבוֹתֵינוּ בִּלְבָד גָּאַל הַקָּדוֹשׁ בָּרוּךְ הוּא, אֶלָּא אַף אוֹתָנוּ גָּאַל עִמָּהֶם, שֶׁנֶּאֱמַר: "וְאוֹתָנוּ הוֹצִיא מִשָּׁם לְמַעַן הָבִיא אֹתָנוּ לָתֶת לָנוּ אֶת הָאָרֶץ אֲשֶׁר נִשְׁבַּע לַאֲבֹתֵינוּ."

B'khol dor vador chayav adam lir'ot et atzmo k'ilu hu yatza miMitzrayim, shene'emar: "V'higadta l'vinkha bayom hahu leimor, ba'avur ze asa Adonai li b'tzeiti miMitzrayim." Lo et avoteinu bilvad ga'al HaKadosh Barukh Hu, ela af otanu ga'al imaham, shene'emar: "V'otanu hotzi misham l'ma'an havi otanu latet lanu et ha'aretz asher nishba la'avoteinu."

In each and every generation, every person is obligated to see themselves as if they left Egypt, as it says: " Because of this *HaShem* did so for *me* when *I* left Egypt." Not only did the Holy One redeem our ancestors, but He redeemed us together with them, as it says: "And He took us out of there in order to bring us to the land which He had promised to our forefathers."

We're almost at the part where we eat, but before we do, we must give thanks for all the miracles we've just recounted.

Lift the cup in your hand, cover the matzah, and recite:

לְפִיכָךְ אֲנַחְנוּ חַיָּבִים לְהוֹדוֹת, לְהַלֵּל, לְשַׁבֵּחַ, לְפָאֵר, לְרוֹמֵם, לְהַדֵּר, לְבָרֵךְ, לְעַלֵּה וּלְקַלֵּס לְמִי שֶׁעָשָׂה לַאֲבוֹתֵינוּ וְלָנוּ אֶת כָּל הַנִּסִּים הָאֵלּוּ: הוֹצִיאָנוּ מֵעַבְדוּת לְחֵרוּת, מִיָּגוֹן לְשִׂמְחָה, וּמֵאֵבֶל לְיוֹם טוֹב, וּמֵאֲפֵלָה לְאוֹר גָּדוֹל, וּמִשִּׁעְבּוּד לִגְאֻלָּה, וְנֹאמַר לְפָנָיו שִׁירָה חֲדָשָׁה, הַלְלוּיָהּ.

L'fikhakh anachnu chayavim l'hodot, l'haleil, l'shabei'ach, l'fa'eir, l'romeim, l'hadeir, l'vareikh, l'alei ulkaleis l'mi she'asa la'avoteinu v'lanu et kol hanisim ha'eilu: Hotzi'anu mei'avdut l'cheirut, miyagon l'simcha, umei'eivel l'yom tov, umei'afeila l'or gadol, umishi'bud lig'ulah, v'nomar l'fanav shira chadasha, hal'luyah.

Therefore we are obligated to thank, praise, laud, glorify, exalt, honor, bless, elevate, and acclaim the One who wrought all these miracles for our ancestors and for us: He brought us out from slavery to freedom, from sorrow to joy, from mourning to feasting, from darkest night to bright light, and from servitude to redemption. So, let us recite a new song before Him, Hallelujah!

הַלְלוּיָהּ הַלְלוּ עַבְדֵי יְהוָה, הַלְלוּ אֶת שֵׁם יְהוָה. יְהִי שֵׁם יְהוָה מְבֹרָךְ, מֵעַתָּה וְעַד עוֹלָם. מִמִּזְרַח שֶׁמֶשׁ עַד מְבוֹאוֹ, מְהֻלָּל שֵׁם יְהוָה. רָם עַל כָּל גּוֹיִם יְהוָה, עַל הַשָּׁמַיִם כְּבוֹדוֹ. מִי כַּיהוָה אֱלֹהֵינוּ הַמַּגְבִּיהִי לָשָׁבֶת, הַמַּשְׁפִּילִי לִרְאוֹת בַּשָּׁמַיִם וּבָאָרֶץ. מְקִימִי מֵעָפָר דָּל, מֵאַשְׁפֹּת יָרִים אֶבְיוֹן. לְהוֹשִׁיבִי עִם נְדִיבִים, עִם נְדִיבֵי עַמּוֹ. מוֹשִׁיבִי עֲקֶרֶת הַבַּיִת, אֵם הַבָּנִים שְׂמֵחָה, הַלְלוּיָהּ.

Hal'luyah hal'lu avdei Adonai, hal'lu et sheim Adonai. Y'hi sheim Adonai m'vorakh, mei'ata v'ad olam. Mimizrach shemesh ad m'vo'o, m'hulal sheim Adonai. Ram al kol goyim Adonai, al hashamayim k'vodo. Mi kAdonai Eloheinu hamagbihi lashavet, hamashpili lir'ot bashamayim uva'aretz. M'kimi mei'afar dal, mei'ashpot yarim evyon. L'hoshivi im n'divim, im n'divei amo. Moshivi akeret habayit, eim habanim s'meicha, hal'luyah.

Hallelujah! Render praise, servants of *HaShem*, praise *HaShem*'s name. May *HaShem*'s name be blessed from now to forever. From the rising of the sun to its setting, may *HaShem*'s name be praised. *HaShem* is exalted above all nations, His glory is above the heavens. Who is like *HaShem*, our God, who sits on high yet gazes down at the heavens and the earth? Who raises the poor out of the dirt, lifts the destitute out of the garbage, to seat him with nobles, the nobles of his people. Who gives the childless woman a household, making her a happy mother of children. Hallelujah!

בְּצֵאת יִשְׂרָאֵל מִמִּצְרָיִם, בֵּית יַעֲקֹב
מֵעַם לֹעֵז. הָיְתָה יְהוּדָה לְקָדְשׁוֹ, יִשְׂרָאֵל
מַמְשְׁלוֹתָיו. הַיָּם רָאָה וַיָּנֹס, הַיַּרְדֵּן יִסֹּב
לְאָחוֹר. הֶהָרִים רָקְדוּ כְאֵילִים, גְּבָעוֹת כִּבְנֵי
צֹאן. מַה לְּךָ הַיָּם כִּי תָנוּס, הַיַּרְדֵּן תִּסֹּב
לְאָחוֹר. הֶהָרִים תִּרְקְדוּ כְאֵילִים, גְּבָעוֹת כִּבְנֵי
צֹאן. מִלִּפְנֵי אָדוֹן חוּלִי אָרֶץ, מִלִּפְנֵי אֱלוֹהַּ
יַעֲקֹב. הַהֹפְכִי הַצּוּר אֲגַם מָיִם, חַלָּמִישׁ
לְמַעְיְנוֹ מָיִם.

B'tzeit Yisra'eil miMitzrayim, beit
Ya'akov mei'am lo'eiz. Hay'ta Y'huda
l'kodsho, Yisra'eil mamsh'lotav.
Hayam ra'a vayanos, haYardein
yisov l'achor. Heharim rak'du kh'eilim,
g'va'ot kivnei tzon. Ma l'kha hayam ki
tanu, haYardein tisov l'achor. Heharim
tirk'du kh'eilim, g'va'ot kivnei tzon.
Milifnei Adon chuli aretz, milifnei
Elo'ah Ya'akov. Hahof'khi hatzur agam
mayim, chalamish l'ma'y'no mayim.

When Israel left Egypt, the house of Jacob left speakers of a strange language. Judah became His holy one, Israel His dominion. The sea saw and fled, the Jordan reversed course. The mountains skipped like rams, the hills like lambs. What alarms you, sea, that you flee, Jordan that you reverse course, mountains that you skip like rams, hills like lambs? Tremble, earth, in the presence of the Lord, in the presence of Jacob's God, who turns the boulder into a pool, the flint into a fountain.

Some Food.

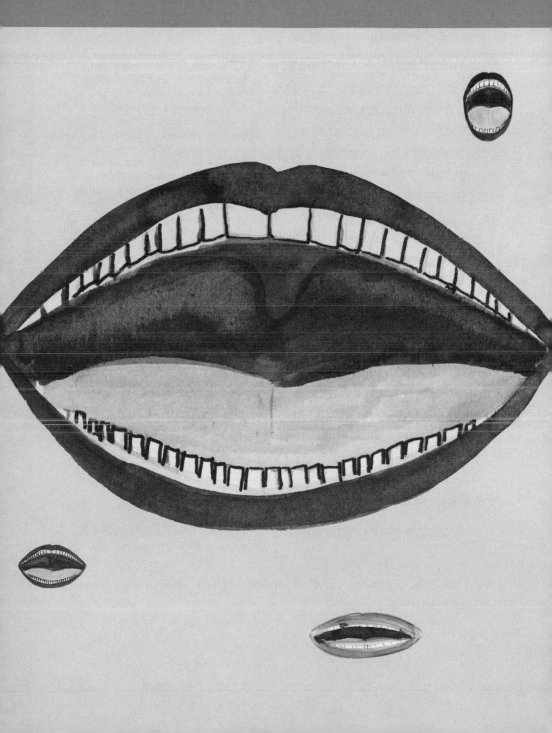

THE · SECOND · CUP

Raise your cup and recite before drinking:

בָּרוּךְ אַתָּה יְהֹוָה אֱלֹהֵינוּ מֶלֶךְ הָעוֹלָם, אֲשֶׁר גְּאָלָנוּ וְגָאַל אֶת אֲבוֹתֵינוּ מִמִּצְרַיִם, וְהִגִּיעָנוּ הַלַּיְלָה הַזֶּה לֶאֱכָל בּוֹ מַצָּה וּמָרוֹר. כֵּן יְהֹוָה אֱלֹהֵינוּ וֵאלֹהֵי אֲבוֹתֵינוּ יַגִּיעֵנוּ לְמוֹעֲדִים וְלִרְגָלִים אֲחֵרִים הַבָּאִים לִקְרָאתֵנוּ לְשָׁלוֹם, שְׂמֵחִים בְּבִנְיַן עִירֶךָ וְשָׂשִׂים בַּעֲבוֹדָתֶךָ, וְנֹאכַל שָׁם מִן הַזְּבָחִים וּמִן הַפְּסָחִים אֲשֶׁר יַגִּיעַ דָּמָם עַל קִיר מִזְבַּחֲךָ לְרָצוֹן, וְנוֹדֶה לְךָ שִׁיר חָדָשׁ עַל גְּאֻלָּתֵנוּ וְעַל פְּדוּת נַפְשֵׁנוּ. בָּרוּךְ אַתָּה יְהֹוָה, גָּאַל יִשְׂרָאֵל.

Barukh ata Adonai Eloheinu melekh ha'olam, asher g'alanu v'ga'al et avoteinu miMitzrayim, v'higi'anu halaila haze le'ekhol bo matzah umaror. Kein Adonai Eloheinu vEilohei avoteinu yagi'einu l'mo'adim v'lirgalim acheirim haba'im likrateinu l'shalom, s'meichim b'vinyan irekha v'sasim ba'avodatekha, v'nokhal sham min haz'vachim umin hap'sachim asher yagi'a damam al kir mizbachakha l'ratzon, v'node l'kha shir chadash al g'ulateinu v'al p'dut nafsheinu. Barukh ata Adonai, ga'al Yisra'eil.

Blessed are You, *HaShem*, our God, Ruler of the Universe, who has redeemed us and redeemed our ancestors from Egypt, and has brought us to this night to eat matzah and *maror*. So, too, *HaShem*, our God and God of our ancestors, bring us to future holidays and festivals in peace and joy at the rebuilding of Your city and with delight in Your worship. We will eat there from the offerings and the Pesach sacrifices, whose blood will reach the wall of your altar for favor. We will thank you with a new song for our redemption and liberation. Blessed are you, *HaShem*, who has redeemed Israel.

After reciting the blessing, drink the second cup while reclining to the left.

בָּרוּךְ אַתָּה יְהֹוָה אֱלֹהֵינוּ מֶלֶךְ הָעוֹלָם, בּוֹרֵא פְּרִי הַגָּפֶן.

Barukh ata Adonai Eloheinu melekh ha'olam, borei p'ri hagafen.

Blessed are You, *HaShem*, our God, Ruler of the Universe, who creates the fruit of the vine.

Rachtzah

Time to wash up again. If you choose to do so, recite the following blessing:

בָּרוּךְ אַתָּה יְהֹוָה אֱלֹהֵינוּ מֶלֶךְ הָעוֹלָם, אֲשֶׁר קִדְּשָׁנוּ בְּמִצְוֹתָיו וְצִוָּנוּ עַל נְטִילַת יָדַיִם.

Barukh ata Adonai Eloheinu melekh ha'olam, asher kid'shanu b'mitzvotav v'tzivanu al n'tilat yadayim.

Blessed are You, *HaShem*, our God, Ruler of the Universe, who has sanctified us with His commandments and given us the commandment of handwashing.

Bless You

Over the course of the evening, we're required to wash our hands twice: once at Urchatz, just before we dip vegetables in salt water, and once now at Rachtzah. But we only say a blessing this time around. Why?

In the Talmud's Tractate Pesachim, Rav Elazar states that one should always wash one's hands before dipping any food item in liquid. Jews being Jews, this seemingly simple statement served as an invitation to a long disputation: Some rabbis argued that Elazar's ruling still applies today, while others claimed that it is just a remnant from the days of the Temple, where the priests had to be pure before performing their duties, and that now that the Temple no longer stands, we're not obligated to be so meticulous.

Enter the halachic principle of Safek Brachot LeHakel: No strangers to stringent rulings, the wise rabbis who shaped Jewish law nonetheless decreed that if there's a *safek*, or doubt, about whether or not you should say a *bracha* in a certain situation, the rabbinic ruling should always strive to opt for the more lenient option. And so, because the rabbis disagreed about whether handwashing before dipping vegetables in liquid was still required, they decided to keep the custom but make things a bit easier by dropping the blessing.

Motzi-Matzah

Remember that small matzah piece? The one you didn't use for the afikoman? Kindly take it and place it between two whole matzahs. Hold them in your hand and recite the following blessings before breaking the top and bottom matzahs into bite-sized pieces and passing them around for your guests to eat (some people lean to the left while eating):

בָּרוּךְ אַתָּה יְהֹוָה אֱלֹהֵינוּ מֶלֶךְ הָעוֹלָם,
הַמּוֹצִיא לֶחֶם מִן הָאָרֶץ.

Barukh ata Adonai Eloheinu melekh ha'olam, hamotzi lechem min ha'aretz.

Blessed are You, *HaShem*, our God, Ruler of the Universe, who brings forth bread from the earth.

בָּרוּךְ אַתָּה יְהֹוָה אֱלֹהֵינוּ מֶלֶךְ הָעוֹלָם, אֲשֶׁר
קִדְּשָׁנוּ בְּמִצְוֹתָיו וְצִוָּנוּ עַל אֲכִילַת מַצָּה.

Barukh ata Adonai Eloheinu melekh ha'olam, asher kid'shanu b'mitzvotav v'tzivanu al akhilat matzah.

Blessed are You, *HaShem*, our God, Ruler of the Universe, who has sanctified us with His commandments and given us the commandment of eating matzah.

Maror

Time for some bitterness—but not too much, because Judaism teaches us that even life's toughest moments are never all dark. Use either a thick piece of fresh horseradish or some of the Romaine lettuce and dip it into the charoset—just enough to slightly sweeten the bite.

בָּרוּךְ אַתָּה יְהֹוָה אֱלֹהֵינוּ מֶלֶךְ הָעוֹלָם, אֲשֶׁר
קִדְּשָׁנוּ בְּמִצְוֹתָיו וְצִוָּנוּ עַל אֲכִילַת מָרוֹר.

Barukh ata Adonai Eloheinu melekh ha'olam, asher kid'shanu b'mitzvotav v'tzivanu al akhilat maror.

Blessed are You, *HaShem*, our God, Ruler of the Universe, who has sanctified us with His commandments and given us the commandment of eating *maror*.

Korekh

Now we take a page from Hillel the Elder and enjoy the whole Passover package by making a sandwich of the matzah and the maror (some people like to add charoset, too) and eating it (some do so while leaning to the left), after reciting the following:

זֵכֶר לְמִקְדָּשׁ כְּהִלֵּל. כֵּן עָשָׂה הִלֵּל בִּזְמַן שֶׁבֵּית הַמִּקְדָּשׁ הָיָה קַיָּם, הָיָה כּוֹרֵךְ פֶּסַח מַצָּה וּמָרוֹר וְאוֹכֵל בְּיַחַד, לְקַיֵּם מַה שֶּׁנֶּאֱמַר: "עַל מַצּוֹת וּמְרוֹרִים יֹאכְלֻהוּ."

Zeikher l'mikdash k'Hilel. Kein asa Hilel bizman sheBeit HaMikdash haya kayam, haya koreikh pesach matzah umaror v'okheil b'yachad, l'kayeim ma shene'emar: "Al matzahs umrorim yokh'luhu."

In memory of the Temple we do as Hillel did when the Temple stood: He would combine the Pesach sacrifice, matzah, and *maror* and eat them together, in order to fulfill what it says: "You should eat it with matzahs and bitter herbs."

The Meal

Leave Your Mark

For many Jews, Haggadot are family heirlooms—and can be living records of each year's memorable conversations, guests, ideas, and more. Those who don't use writing utensils on the holiday can mark up these pages before or after (or both).

The Home Stretch

Afikoman Search

It's time for the kids to go looking for that piece of matzah you hid.
Send them a-searching and let the prize negotiations begin.

The Ultimate Passover Dessert

Every person who keeps kosher for Passover has at some point wondered why things with corn syrup in them—which is to say, things made with corn (which, if you believe Michael Pollan, is pretty much everything)—are not *pesadik*. Well, it's because corn has been known to go into the making of bread, and corn used to be tilled in the same soil as wheat, which also made bread. And bread, and bread-like things, should not be eaten during Passover.

But cookie dough is another matter. It is of course *chametz,* since it invariably contains flour or wheat or something used to make cookies, and said materials invariably were made wet for over the eighteen-minute limit.

But c'mon! Think this through! Cookie dough should be kosher for Passover. It is the *very definition* of what ought to be kosher for Passover: would-be bread that specifically hasn't been baked. It is the precise sort of thing you would grab for a nosh if you didn't have enough time to prepare properly—because, maybe, oh, I dunno, you were fleeing Pharaoh! Eating cookie dough on Passover shouldn't just be countenanced. We should be slathering it on the *afikoman* for dessert.

—*Marc Tracy*

Tzafun: Auction

Once the *afikoman* is retrieved and presented by the children to the Seder's leader, he or she must negotiate a small payment for its return. Some families offer fancy presents; others, symbolic gifts. You do you. Once the *afikoman* has been redeemed, give a little piece of it to each guest to eat. From this point on, it is forbidden to eat anything else.

There are still two cups of wine left to drink, though....

Barekh

Traditionally, this is where we say a blessing to thank God for the meal we've just enjoyed. There is also an additional approach: Have every person around your table speak from the heart and bless the person sitting next to them.

LEAPFROG

The next big moment is the Third Cup (page 91).

Pour the third cup of wine and recite Birkat Hamazon (Blessing after the Meal).

שִׁיר הַמַּעֲלוֹת: בְּשׁוּב יְהֹוָה אֶת שִׁיבַת צִיּוֹן הָיִינוּ כְּחֹלְמִים. אָז יִמָּלֵא שְׂחוֹק פִּינוּ וּלְשׁוֹנֵנוּ רִנָּה, אָז יֹאמְרוּ בַגּוֹיִם, הִגְדִּיל יְהֹוָה לַעֲשׂוֹת עִם אֵלֶּה. הִגְדִּיל יְהֹוָה לַעֲשׂוֹת עִמָּנוּ, הָיִינוּ שְׂמֵחִים. שׁוּבָה יְהֹוָה אֶת שְׁבִיתֵנוּ, כַּאֲפִיקִים בַּנֶּגֶב. הַזֹּרְעִים בְּדִמְעָה בְּרִנָּה יִקְצֹרוּ. הָלוֹךְ יֵלֵךְ וּבָכֹה נֹשֵׂא מֶשֶׁךְ הַזָּרַע, בֹּא יָבֹא בְרִנָּה נֹשֵׂא אֲלֻמֹּתָיו.

Shir hama'alot: B'shuv Adonai et shivat Tziyon hayinu k'chol'mim. Az yimalei s'chok pinu ulshoneinu rina, az yom'ru vagoyim, higdil Adonai la'asot im eile. Higdil Adonai la'asot imanu, hayinu s'meichim. Shuva Adonai et sh'viteinu, ka'afikim baNegev. Hazor'im b'dim'a b'rina yiktzoru. Halokh yeileikh uvakho nosei meshekh hazara, bo yavo v'rina nosei alumotav.

תְּהִלַּת יְהֹוָה יְדַבֶּר פִּי, וִיבָרֵךְ כָּל בָּשָׂר שֵׁם קָדְשׁוֹ לְעוֹלָם וָעֶד. וַאֲנַחְנוּ נְבָרֵךְ יָהּ מֵעַתָּה וְעַד עוֹלָם הַלְלוּיָהּ. הוֹדוּ לַיהֹוָה כִּי טוֹב כִּי לְעוֹלָם חַסְדּוֹ. מִי יְמַלֵּל גְּבוּרוֹת יְהֹוָה יַשְׁמִיעַ כָּל תְּהִלָּתוֹ.

T'hilat Adonai y'daber pi, vivareikh kol basar sheim kodsho l'olam va'ed. Va'anachnu n'vareikh Yah mei'ata v'ad olam hal'luyah. Hodu lAdonai ki tov ki l'olam chasdo. Mi y'maleil g'vurot Adonai yashmi'a kol t'hilato.

A song of ascents: When *HaShem* returns Zion's exiles, we will be like dreamers. Our mouths will be full of laughter and our tongues with melodies. It will be said around the world: "*HaShem* has done great things for them." *HaShem* has done great things for us, and we will rejoice. *HaShem*, bring back our captives like streams in the desert. Those who sow in tears will reap in joy. Though the farmer walks along bearing the measure of seed in tears, he will come home bearing his sheaves with joy.

Let my mouth declare *HaShem*'s praise, let all flesh bless His holy name forever. We will bless *HaShem* forever and ever, Hallelujah!

Give thanks to *HaShem* for He is good, for His kindness is eternal. Who can express *HaShem*'s mighty deeds or exhaust His praise?

Include the following and any words in parentheses when there is a minyan, or ten Jews, present.

Leader:

רַבּוֹתַי נְבָרֵךְ.

Rabotai n'var'kh.

Friends, let us say grace.

יְהִי שֵׁם יְהֹוָה מְבֹרָךְ מֵעַתָּה וְעַד עוֹלָם.

Y'hi sheim Adonai m'vorakh mei'ata v'ad olam.

Let *HaShem*'s name be blessed now and forever.

Leader:

יְהִי שֵׁם יְהֹוָה מְבֹרָךְ מֵעַתָּה וְעַד עוֹלָם. בִּרְשׁוּת מָרָנָן וְרַבָּנָן וְרַבּוֹתַי נְבָרֵךְ (אֱלֹהֵינוּ) שֶׁאָכַלְנוּ מִשֶּׁלוֹ.

Y'hi sheim Adonai m'vorakh mei'ata v'ad olam, Birshut maranan v'rabanan v'rabotai n'varekh (Eloheinu) she'akhalnu mishelo.

Let *HaShem*'s name be blessed now and forever. With your permission, let us now bless (our God) whose food we have eaten.

Participants:

בָּרוּךְ (אֱלֹהֵינוּ) שֶׁאָכַלְנוּ מִשֶּׁלוֹ וּבְטוּבוֹ חָיִּינוּ.

Barukh (Eloheinu) she'akhalnu mishelo uvtuvo chayinu.

Blessed be (our God) whose food we have eaten and by whose beneficence we live.

Leader:

בָּרוּךְ (אֱלֹהֵינוּ) שֶׁאָכַלְנוּ מִשֶּׁלוֹ וּבְטוּבוֹ חָיִּינוּ.

Barukh (Eloheinu) she'akhalnu mishelo uvtuvo chayinu.

Blessed be (our God) whose food we have eaten and by whose beneficence we live.

בָּרוּךְ הוּא וּבָרוּךְ שְׁמוֹ.

Barukh hu uvarukh sh'mo.

Blessed be He and blessed be His name.

Continue here if there isn't a minyan, or ten Jews, present.

בָּרוּךְ אַתָּה יְהֹוָה אֱלֹהֵינוּ מֶלֶךְ הָעוֹלָם,
הַזָּן אֶת הָעוֹלָם כֻּלּוֹ בְּטוּבוֹ, בְּחֵן בְּחֶסֶד
וּבְרַחֲמִים, הוּא נוֹתֵן לֶחֶם לְכָל בָּשָׂר, כִּי
לְעוֹלָם חַסְדּוֹ. וּבְטוּבוֹ הַגָּדוֹל תָּמִיד לֹא חָסַר
לָנוּ וְאַל יֶחְסַר לָנוּ מָזוֹן לְעוֹלָם וָעֶד. בַּעֲבוּר
שְׁמוֹ הַגָּדוֹל, כִּי הוּא אֵל זָן וּמְפַרְנֵס לַכֹּל,
וּמֵטִיב לַכֹּל וּמֵכִין מָזוֹן לְכָל בְּרִיּוֹתָיו אֲשֶׁר
בָּרָא. בָּרוּךְ אַתָּה יְהֹוָה, הַזָּן אֶת הַכֹּל.

Barukh ata Adonai Eloheinu melekh
ha'olam, hazan et ha'olam kulo
b'tuvo, b'chein b'chesed uvrachamim,
hu notein lechem l'khol basar, ki
l'olam chasdo. Uvtuvo hagadol tamid
lo chasar lanu v'al yechsar lanu
mazon l'olam va'ed. Ba'avur sh'mo
hagadol, ki hu El zan umfarneis lakol,
umeitiv lakol umeikhin mazon l'khol
b'riyotav asher bara. Barukh ata
Adonai, hazan et hakol.

Blessed are You, *HaShem*, our God, Ruler of the Universe, who nourishes the whole world in His goodness—with grace, with kindness, and with mercy. He gives food to all flesh, for His kindness endures forever. On account of His great beneficence we have never been lacking, and may we never ever lack nourishment, for the sake of His great name. Because He is God who nourishes and sustains all, and benefits all, and provides nourishment for all of the creatures He has created. Blessed are You, *HaShem*, who nourishes all.

נוֹדֶה לְךָ יְהֹוָה אֱלֹהֵינוּ עַל שֶׁהִנְחַלְתָּ
לַאֲבוֹתֵינוּ אֶרֶץ חֶמְדָּה טוֹבָה וּרְחָבָה, וְעַל
שֶׁהוֹצֵאתָנוּ יְהֹוָה אֱלֹהֵינוּ מֵאֶרֶץ מִצְרַיִם
וּפְדִיתָנוּ מִבֵּית עֲבָדִים, וְעַל בְּרִיתְךָ שֶׁחָתַמְתָּ
בִּבְשָׂרֵנוּ, וְעַל תּוֹרָתְךָ שֶׁלִּמַּדְתָּנוּ, וְעַל חֻקֶּיךָ
שֶׁהוֹדַעְתָּנוּ, וְעַל חַיִּים חֵן וָחֶסֶד שֶׁחוֹנַנְתָּנוּ,
וְעַל אֲכִילַת מָזוֹן שָׁאַתָּה זָן וּמְפַרְנֵס אוֹתָנוּ
תָּמִיד בְּכָל יוֹם וּבְכָל עֵת וּבְכָל שָׁעָה.

Node l'kha Adonai Eloheinu al
shehinchalta la'avoteinu eretz chemda
tova urchava, v'al shehotzeitanu
Adonai Eloheinu mei'eretz Mitzrayim
ufditanu mibeit avadim, v'al b'rit'kha
shechatamta bivsareinu, v'al
Torat'kha shelimadtanu, v'al chukekha
shehoda'tanu, v'al chayim chein
vachesed shechonantanu, v'al akhilat
mazon she'ata zan umfarneis otanu
tamid b'khol yom uvkhol eit uvkhol
sha'a.

We thank You, *HaShem*, our God, for having granted our forefathers a desirable, good, and spacious land; for having taken us out from the land of Egypt and having redeemed us from the house of bondage; for Your covenant which You sealed in our bodies; for Your Torah which You taught us; for Your laws of which you informed us; for the life, grace, and kindness which You have granted us; and for the provision of food with which You nourish and sustain us constantly—every second of the day.

וְעַל הַכֹּל יְהֹוָה אֱלֹהֵינוּ אֲנַחְנוּ מוֹדִים לָךְ וּמְבָרְכִים אוֹתָךְ יִתְבָּרַךְ שִׁמְךָ בְּפִי כָל חַי תָּמִיד לְעוֹלָם וָעֶד. כַּכָּתוּב: וְאָכַלְתָּ וְשָׂבָעְתָּ וּבֵרַכְתָּ אֶת יְהֹוָה אֱלֹהֶיךָ עַל הָאָרֶץ הַטֹּבָה אֲשֶׁר נָתַן לָךְ. בָּרוּךְ אַתָּה יְהֹוָה, עַל הָאָרֶץ וְעַל הַמָּזוֹן.

V'al hakol Adonai Eloheinu anachnu modim lakh umvar'khim otakh yitbarakh shimkha b'fi kol chai tamid l'olam va'ed. Kakatuv: V'akhalta v'sava'ta uveirakhta et Adonai Elohekha al ha'aretz hatova asher natan lakh. Barukh ata Adonai, al ha'aretz v'al hamazon.

For everything, *HaShem*, our God, we thank and bless You. May the blessedness of your name be on the lips of every living thing forever, as it is written: "After you have eaten and are satisfied, you will bless *HaShem*, your God, for the good land He has given you." Blessed are You, *HaShem*, for the land and the food.

רַחֵם נָא יְהֹוָה אֱלֹהֵינוּ עַל יִשְׂרָאֵל עַמֶּךָ, וְעַל יְרוּשָׁלַיִם עִירֶךָ, וְעַל צִיּוֹן מִשְׁכַּן כְּבוֹדֶךָ, וְעַל מַלְכוּת בֵּית דָּוִד מְשִׁיחֶךָ, וְעַל הַבַּיִת הַגָּדוֹל וְהַקָּדוֹשׁ שֶׁנִּקְרָא שִׁמְךָ עָלָיו. אֱלֹהֵינוּ אָבִינוּ רְעֵנוּ זוּנֵנוּ פַּרְנְסֵנוּ וְכַלְכְּלֵנוּ וְהַרְוִיחֵנוּ וְהַרְוַח לָנוּ יְהֹוָה אֱלֹהֵינוּ מְהֵרָה מִכָּל צָרוֹתֵינוּ. וְנָא אַל תַּצְרִיכֵנוּ יְהֹוָה אֱלֹהֵינוּ לֹא לִידֵי מַתְּנַת בָּשָׂר וָדָם וְלֹא לִידֵי הַלְוָאָתָם, כִּי אִם לְיָדְךָ הַמְּלֵאָה הַפְּתוּחָה הַקְּדוֹשָׁה וְהָרְחָבָה, שֶׁלֹּא נֵבוֹשׁ וְלֹא נִכָּלֵם לְעוֹלָם וָעֶד.

Racheim na Adonai Eloheinu al Yisra'eil amekha, v'al Y'rushalayim irekha, v'al Tziyon mishkan k'vodekha, v'al malkhut beit David m'shichekha, v'al habayit hagadol v'hakadosh shenikra shimkha alav. Eloheinu avinu r'einu zuneinu parn'seinu v'khalk'leinu v'harvicheinu v'harvach lanu Adonai Eloheinu m'heira mikol tzaroteinu. V'na al tatzrikheinu Adonai Eloheinu lo lidei matnat basar vadam v'lo lidei halva'atam, ki im l'yad'kha ham'lei'a hap'tucha hak'dosha v'har'chava, shelo neivosh v'lo nikaleim l'olam va'ed.

Have mercy, *HaShem*, our God, on Israel Your people, on Jerusalem Your city, on Zion the abode of Your glory, on the kingdom of the house of David Your anointed, and on the great and holy Temple that bears Your name. Our God, our Father, tend us, feed us, sustain us, support us, relieve us. Speedily, *HaShem*, our God, grant us relief from all our troubles. *HaShem*, our God, do not make us rely on the gifts and loans of men but rather on your full, open, and generous hand, so that we may never be put to shame and disgrace.

רְצֵה וְהַחֲלִיצֵנוּ יְהֹוָה אֱלֹהֵינוּ בְּמִצְוֹתֶיךָ
וּבְמִצְוַת יוֹם הַשְּׁבִיעִי, הַשַּׁבָּת הַגָּדוֹל וְהַקָּדוֹשׁ
הַזֶּה, כִּי יוֹם זֶה גָּדוֹל וְקָדוֹשׁ הוּא לְפָנֶיךָ
לִשְׁבָּת בּוֹ וְלָנוּחַ בּוֹ בְּאַהֲבָה כְּמִצְוַת רְצוֹנֶךָ,
וּבִרְצוֹנְךָ הָנִיחַ לָנוּ יְהֹוָה אֱלֹהֵינוּ שֶׁלֹּא תְהֵא
צָרָה וְיָגוֹן וַאֲנָחָה בְּיוֹם מְנוּחָתֵנוּ, וְהַרְאֵנוּ
יְהֹוָה אֱלֹהֵינוּ בְּנֶחָמַת צִיּוֹן עִירֶךָ וּבְבִנְיַן
יְרוּשָׁלַיִם עִיר קָדְשֶׁךָ, כִּי אַתָּה הוּא בַּעַל
הַיְשׁוּעוֹת וּבַעַל הַנֶּחָמוֹת.

R'tzei v'hachalitzeinu Adonai Eloheinu b'mitzvotekha uvmitzvat yom hash'vi'i, haShabbat hagadol v'hakadosh haze, ki yom ze gadol v'kadosh hu l'fanekha lishbot bo v'lanu'ach bo b'ahava k'mitzvat r'tzonekha, uvirtzon'kha hani'ach lanu Adonai Eloheinu shelo t'hei tzara v'yagon va'anacha b'yom m'nuchateinu, v'har'einu Adonai Eloheinu b'nechmat Tziyon irekha uv'vinyan Y'rushalayim ir kodshekha, ki ata hu ba'al hayshu'ot uva'al hanechamot.

Favor us and strengthen us, *HaShem*, our God, with Your commandments, and with the commandment concerning the seventh day, this great and holy Shabbat. This day is great and holy before You to abstain from work and rest on it in love, according to your will. May it be Your will, *HaShem*, our God, to grant us rest so that there be no trouble, grief, or lament on our day of rest. *HaShem*, our God, let us live to see Zion Your city comforted, Jerusalem Your holy city rebuilt, for You are the Master of all salvation and consolation.

אֱלֹהֵינוּ וֵאלֹהֵי אֲבוֹתֵינוּ, יַעֲלֶה וְיָבֹא וְיַגִּיעַ
וְיֵרָאֶה וְיֵרָצֶה וְיִשָּׁמַע וְיִפָּקֵד וְיִזָּכֵר זִכְרוֹנֵנוּ
וּפִקְדוֹנֵנוּ, וְזִכְרוֹן אֲבוֹתֵינוּ, וְזִכְרוֹן מָשִׁיחַ
בֶּן דָּוִד עַבְדֶּךָ, וְזִכְרוֹן יְרוּשָׁלַיִם עִיר קָדְשֶׁךָ,
וְזִכְרוֹן כָּל עַמְּךָ בֵּית יִשְׂרָאֵל לְפָנֶיךָ, לִפְלֵיטָה
לְטוֹבָה לְחֵן וּלְחֶסֶד וּלְרַחֲמִים, לְחַיִּים
וּלְשָׁלוֹם בְּיוֹם חַג הַמַּצּוֹת הַזֶּה. זָכְרֵנוּ
יְהֹוָה אֱלֹהֵינוּ בּוֹ לְטוֹבָה וּפָקְדֵנוּ בוֹ לִבְרָכָה
וְהוֹשִׁיעֵנוּ בוֹ לְחַיִּים. וּבִדְבַר יְשׁוּעָה וְרַחֲמִים
חוּס וְחָנֵּנוּ וְרַחֵם עָלֵינוּ וְהוֹשִׁיעֵנוּ, כִּי אֵלֶיךָ
עֵינֵינוּ, כִּי אֵל מֶלֶךְ חַנּוּן וְרַחוּם אָתָּה.

Eloheinu vEilohei avoteinu, ya'ale v'yavo v'yagi'a v'yeira'e v'yeiratze v'yishama v'yipakeid v'yizakheir zikhroneinu ufikdoneinu, v'zikhron avoteinu, v'zikhron Mashi'ach ben David avdekha, v'zikhron Y'rushalayim ir kodshekha, v'zikhron kol am'kha beit Yisra'eil l'fanekha, lifleita l'lova l'chein ulchesed ulrachamim, l'chayim ulshalom b'yom Chag Hamatzot haze. Zokhreinu Adonai Eloheinu bo l'tova ufokdeinu vo livrakha v'hoshi'einu vo l'chayim. Uvidvar y'shu'a v'rachamim chus v'choneinu v'racheim aleinu v'hoshi'einu, ki eilekha eineinu, ki Eil melekh chanun v'rachum ata.

Our God and the God of our forefathers, may the remembrance of us, of our fathers, of the Messiah son of David Your servant, of Jerusalem

Your holy city, and of all Your people the House of Israel, ascend, come, and reach You, be noticed, favored, heard, considered, and remembered before You, for deliverance and goodness, for grace, kindness, and mercy, for life and peace, on this day of the Festival of Matzahs. Remember us *HaShem*, our God, on this day for goodness; consider us on it for blessing; save us on it for life. With a word of salvation and mercy spare us and favor us, have pity on us and save us, for we look to You, for You are a gracious and merciful God and Ruler.

וּבְנֵה יְרוּשָׁלַיִם עִיר הַקֹּדֶשׁ בִּמְהֵרָה בְיָמֵינוּ. בָּרוּךְ אַתָּה יְהֹוָה, בּוֹנֵה בְרַחֲמָיו יְרוּשָׁלָיִם. אָמֵן.

Uvnei Y'rushalayim ir hakodesh bimheira v'yameinu. Barukh ata Adonai, bonei v'rachamav Y'rushalayim. Amein.

Rebuild Jerusalem the holy city speedily in our days. Blessed are You, *HaShem*, who rebuilds Jerusalem in His mercy. Amen.

בָּרוּךְ אַתָּה יְהֹוָה אֱלֹהֵינוּ מֶלֶךְ הָעוֹלָם, הָאֵל אָבִינוּ מַלְכֵּנוּ אַדִּירֵנוּ בּוֹרְאֵנוּ גֹּאֲלֵנוּ יוֹצְרֵנוּ קְדוֹשֵׁנוּ קְדוֹשׁ יַעֲקֹב, רוֹעֵנוּ רוֹעֵה יִשְׂרָאֵל, הַמֶּלֶךְ הַטּוֹב וְהַמֵּטִיב לַכֹּל, שֶׁבְּכָל יוֹם וָיוֹם הוּא הֵטִיב הוּא מֵטִיב הוּא יֵיטִיב לָנוּ, הוּא גְמָלָנוּ הוּא גוֹמְלֵנוּ הוּא יִגְמְלֵנוּ לָעַד, לְחֵן וּלְחֶסֶד וּלְרַחֲמִים וּלְרֶוַח הַצָּלָה וְהַצְלָחָה בְּרָכָה וִישׁוּעָה נֶחָמָה פַּרְנָסָה וְכַלְכָּלָה וְרַחֲמִים וְחַיִּים וְשָׁלוֹם וְכָל טוֹב, וּמִכָּל טוּב לְעוֹלָם אַל יְחַסְּרֵנוּ.

Barukh ata Adonai Eloheinu melekh ha'olam, ha'El avinu malkeinu adireinu bor'einu go'aleinu yotz'reinu k'dosheinu k'dosh Ya'akov, ro'einu ro'e Yisra'eil, hamelekh hatov v'hameitiv lakol, sheb'khol yom vayom hu heitiv hu meitiv hu yeitiv lanu, hu g'malanu hu gom'leinu hu yigm'leinu la'ad, l'chein ulchesed ulrachamim ulrevach hatzala v'hatzlacha b'rakha vishu'a nechama parnasa v'khalkala v'rachamim v'chayim v'shalom v'khol tov, umikol tuv l'olam al y'chas'reinu.

Blessed are You, *HaShem*, our God, Ruler of the Universe, the God who is our Father, our Ruler, our Sovereign, our Creator, our Redeemer, our Maker, our Holy One, the Holy One of Jacob, the Shepherd of Israel, the good Ruler who does good to all and has done good, does good, and will do good to us every single day. He has been bountiful, is bountiful, and will forever be bountiful with us, with grace, kindness and mercy, relief and deliverance, success, blessing, salvation, comfort, sustenance, support, mercy, life and peace and all goodness. May He never deprive us of any good.

הָרַחֲמָן הוּא יִמְלֹךְ עָלֵינוּ לְעוֹלָם וָעֶד.

HaRachaman hu yimlokh aleinu l'olam va'ed.

הָרַחֲמָן הוּא יִתְבָּרַךְ בַּשָּׁמַיִם וּבָאָרֶץ.

HaRachaman hu yitbarakh bashamayim uva'aretz.

הָרַחֲמָן הוּא יִשְׁתַּבַּח לְדוֹר דּוֹרִים וְיִתְפָּאַר בָּנוּ לָעַד וּלְנֵצַח נְצָחִים, וְיִתְהַדַּר בָּנוּ לָעַד וּלְעוֹלְמֵי עוֹלָמִים.

HaRachaman hu yishtabach l'dor dorim v'yitpa'ar banu la'ad ulneitzach n'tzachim, v'yit-hadar banu la'ad ulol'mei olamim.

הָרַחֲמָן הוּא יְפַרְנְסֵנוּ בְּכָבוֹד.

HaRachaman hu y'farn'seinu b'khavod.

הָרַחֲמָן הוּא יִשְׁבֹּר עֻלֵּנוּ מֵעַל צַוָּארֵנוּ וְהוּא יוֹלִיכֵנוּ קוֹמְמִיּוּת לְאַרְצֵנוּ.

HaRachaman hu yishbor uleinu mei'al tzavareinu v'hu yolikheinu kom'miyut l'artzeinu.

הָרַחֲמָן הוּא יִשְׁלַח לָנוּ בְּרָכָה מְרֻבָּה בַּבַּיִת הַזֶּה וְעַל שֻׁלְחָן זֶה שֶׁאָכַלְנוּ עָלָיו.

HaRachaman hu yishlach lanu b'rakha m'ruba babayit haze v'al shulchan ze she'akhalnu alav.

הָרַחֲמָן הוּא יִשְׁלַח לָנוּ אֶת אֵלִיָּהוּ הַנָּבִיא זָכוּר לַטּוֹב וִיבַשֶּׂר לָנוּ בְּשׂוֹרוֹת טוֹבוֹת יְשׁוּעוֹת וְנֶחָמוֹת.

HaRachaman hu yishlach lanu et Eiliyahu hanavi zakhur latov vivaser lanu b'sorot tovot y'shu'ot v'nechamot.

May the Merciful One rule over us forever and ever.

May the Merciful One be blessed in heaven and on earth.

May the Merciful One be praised for all generations; may He be glorified through us for all time; may He be honored through us for all eternity.

May the Merciful One sustain in dignity.

May the Merciful One break the yoke around our neck and lead us with our heads held high into our land.

May the Merciful One send abundant blessing into this house and onto this table at which we have eaten.

May the Merciful One send us the prophet Elijah of blessed memory to bring us good tidings of salvation and consolation.

הָרַחֲמָן הוּא יְבָרֵךְ אֶת

HaRachaman hu y'vareikh et

May the Merciful One bless

For one's hosts (and parents), add:

(אָבִי מוֹרִי) בַּעַל הַבַּיִת הַזֶּה וְאֶת (אִמִּי מוֹרָתִי) בַּעֲלַת הַבַּיִת הַזֶּה, אוֹתָם וְאֶת בֵּיתָם וְאֶת זַרְעָם וְאֶת כָּל אֲשֶׁר לָהֶם,

(for one's father add: avi mori) ba'al habayit haze v'et (for one's mother add: imi morati) ba'alat habayit haze, otam v'et beitam v'et zar'am v'et kol asher lahem,

(my revered father) the master of this house and (my revered mother) the mistress of this house, them, and their household, and their children, and everything that is theirs,

GIVE IT UP FOR GRANDPA

For one's family, add:

אוֹתִי (וְאֶת אִשְׁתִּי/בַּעֲלִי/זַרְעִי) וְאֶת כָּל אֲשֶׁר לִי,

oti (v'et ishti/ba'ali/zar'i) v'et kol asher li,

me (and my wife/husband/children) and all that is mine,

LOVE YOU, FAM

For all others, add:

ALSO YOU, FIDO

וְאֶת כָּל הַמְסֻבִּין כָּאן,

v'et kol ham'subin kan,

and all who are seated here,

AND AND AND

אוֹתָנוּ וְאֶת כָּל אֲשֶׁר לָנוּ, כְּמוֹ שֶׁנִּתְבָּרְכוּ אֲבוֹתֵינוּ אַבְרָהָם יִצְחָק וְיַעֲקֹב בַּכֹּל מִכֹּל כֹּל, כֵּן יְבָרֵךְ אוֹתָנוּ כֻּלָּנוּ יַחַד בִּבְרָכָה שְׁלֵמָה, וְנֹאמַר אָמֵן.

otanu v'et kol asher lanu, k'mo shenitbar'khu avoteinu Avraham Yitzchak v'Ya'akov bakol mikol kol, kein y'vareikh otanu kulanu yachad bivrakha sh'leima, v'nomar amein.

us and all our possessions. Just as He blessed our forefathers Abraham, Isaac, and Jacob with every blessing, so may He bless us all together with a complete blessing, and let us say: Amen.

בַּמָּרוֹם יְלַמְּדוּ עֲלֵיהֶם וְעָלֵינוּ זְכוּת שֶׁתְּהֵא לְמִשְׁמֶרֶת שָׁלוֹם, וְנִשָּׂא בְרָכָה מֵאֵת יְהֹוָה וּצְדָקָה מֵאֱלֹהֵי יִשְׁעֵנוּ, וְנִמְצָא חֵן וְשֵׂכֶל טוֹב בְּעֵינֵי אֱלֹהִים וְאָדָם.

Bamarom y'lam'du aleihem v'aleinu z'khut shet'hei l'mishmeret shalom, v'nisa v'rakha mei'eit Adonai utzdaka mei'Elohei yish'einu, v'nimtza chein v'seikhel tov b'einei Elohim v'adam.

May heaven find merit in us that we may enjoy a lasting peace. May we receive blessings from *HaShem* and justice from the God of our salvation, and may we find favor and approbation in the eyes of God and man.

On Shabbat add:

הָרַחֲמָן הוּא יַנְחִילֵנוּ יוֹם שֶׁכֻּלּוֹ שַׁבָּת וּמְנוּחָה לְחַיֵּי הָעוֹלָמִים.

HaRachaman hu yanchileinu yom shekulo Shabbat umnucha l'chayei ha'olamim.

May the Merciful One cause us to inherit the time which will be entirely Shabbat and eternal repose.

הָרַחֲמָן הוּא יַנְחִילֵנוּ יוֹם שֶׁכֻּלּוֹ טוֹב.

HaRachaman hu yanchileinu yom shekulo tov.

May the Merciful One cause us to inherit the time of absolute goodness.

הָרַחֲמָן הוּא יְזַכֵּנוּ לִימוֹת הַמָּשִׁיחַ וּלְחַיֵּי הָעוֹלָם הַבָּא. מִגְדּוֹל יְשׁוּעוֹת מַלְכּוֹ וְעֹשֶׂה חֶסֶד לִמְשִׁיחוֹ לְדָוִד וּלְזַרְעוֹ עַד עוֹלָם. עֹשֶׂה שָׁלוֹם בִּמְרוֹמָיו הוּא יַעֲשֶׂה שָׁלוֹם עָלֵינוּ וְעַל כָּל יִשְׂרָאֵל, וְאִמְרוּ אָמֵן.

HaRachaman hu y'zakeinu limot hamashi'ach ulchayei ha'olam haba. Migdol y'shu'ot malko v'ose chesed limshisho l'David ulzar'o ad olam. Ose Shalom Bimromav hu ya'ase shalom aleinu v'al kol Yisra'eil, v'imru amein.

May the Merciful One make us worthy of the messianic period and the World to Come. God is a tower of salvation to His king, showing kindness to His anointed, to David and his descendants forever. May the One who makes peace on high make peace for us and all Israel, and let us say: amen.

יְראוּ אֶת יְהֹוָה קְדֹשָׁיו, כִּי אֵין מַחְסוֹר לִירֵאָיו. כְּפִירִים רָשׁוּ וְרָעֵבוּ, וְדֹרְשֵׁי יְהֹוָה לֹא יַחְסְרוּ כָל טוֹב. הוֹדוּ לַיהֹוָה כִּי טוֹב, כִּי לְעוֹלָם חַסְדּוֹ. פּוֹתֵחַ אֶת יָדֶךָ וּמַשְׂבִּיעַ לְכָל חַי רָצוֹן. בָּרוּךְ הַגֶּבֶר אֲשֶׁר יִבְטַח בַּיהֹוָה, וְהָיָה יְהֹוָה מִבְטַחוֹ. נַעַר הָיִיתִי גַם זָקַנְתִּי, וְלֹא רָאִיתִי צַדִּיק נֶעֱזָב וְזַרְעוֹ מְבַקֶּשׁ לָחֶם. יְהֹוָה עֹז לְעַמּוֹ יִתֵּן, יְהֹוָה יְבָרֵךְ אֶת עַמּוֹ בַשָּׁלוֹם.

Y'ru et Adonai k'doshav, ki ein machsor lirei'av. K'firim rashu v'ra'eivu, v'dor'shei Adonai lo yachs'ru khol tov. Hodu lAdonai ki tov, ki l'olam chasdo. Pote'ach et yadekha umasbi'a l'khol chai ratzon. Barukh hagever asher yivtach bAdonai, v'haya Adonai mivtacho. Na'ar hayiti gam zakanti, v'lo ra'iti tzadik ne'ezav v'zar'o m'vakesh lachem. Adonai oz l'amo yitein, Adonai y'vareikh et amo vashalom.

Revere *HaShem*, His holy ones, for those who revere him suffer no want. Young lions may be wasting away, but those who seek the Lord will not lack any good. Give thanks to *HaShem*, for He is good; His kindness endures forever. You open Your hand and satisfy the desire of every living thing. Blessed are those who trust in *HaShem*, so that *HaShem* becomes their security. Neither in my youth or old age have I ever seen the righteous forsaken, their children begging for bread. May *HaShem* give strength to His people; may *HaShem* bless His people with peace.

Optional blessings:

הָרַחֲמָן הוּא יְבָרֵךְ אֶת מְדִינַת יִשְׂרָאֵל.

HaRachaman hu y'vareikh et m'dinat Yisra'eil.

הָרַחֲמָן הוּא יְבָרֵךְ אֶת חַיְּלֵי צְבָא הַהֲגַנָּה לְיִשְׂרָאֵל וְיָגֵן עֲלֵיהֶם.

HaRachaman hu y'vareikh et chayalei Tz'va haHagana l'Yisra'eil v'yagein aleihem.

הָרַחֲמָן הוּא יְבָרֵךְ אֶת הַמְּדִינָה הַזֹּאת וְאֶת חַיָלֶיהָ וְיָגֵן עֲלֵיהֶם.

HaRachaman hu y'vareikh et ham'dina hazot v'et chayaleha v'yagein aleihem.

הָרַחֲמָן הוּא יַשְׁכִּין שָׁלוֹם בֵּין בְּנֵי יַעֲקֹב וּבְנֵי יִשְׁמָעֵאל.

HaRachaman hu yashkin shalom bein b'nei Ya'akov uvnei Yishma'eil.

May the Merciful One bless the State of Israel.

May the Merciful One bless those who serve in the IDF and protect them.

May the Merciful One bless this country and its soldiers and protect them.

May the Merciful One bring peace between the descendants of Jacob and the descendants of Ishmael.

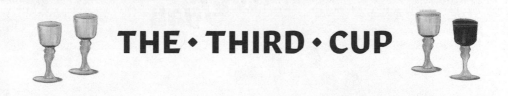

THE · THIRD · CUP

Raise that third cup of wine, say the following blessing, and drink. Some people recline to the left as they do so:

בָּרוּךְ אַתָּה יְהוָֹה אֱלֹהֵינוּ מֶלֶךְ הָעוֹלָם, בּוֹרֵא פְּרִי הַגָּפֶן.

Barukh ata Adonai Eloheinu melekh ha'olam, borei p'ri hagafen.

Blessed are You, *HaShem*, our God, Ruler of the Universe, who creates the fruit of the vine.

Grab the fanciest goblet-like cup you've got, fill it with wine, and open the door to welcome in the prophet Elijah.

Elijah's Cup

Traditionally the youngest children open the door for Elijah. Everyone joins in singing "Eliyahu Ha-Navi," and then the door is closed.

Why? Because the whole point of the Seder is to make sure everyone understands that redemption isn't an abstract concept—it's a distinct possibility, something to work toward and believe in.

אֵלִיָּהוּ הַנָּבִיא, אֵלִיָּהוּ הַתִּשְׁבִּי, אֵלִיָּהוּ הַגִּלְעָדִי, בִּמְהֵרָה יָבוֹא אֵלֵינוּ עִם מָשִׁיחַ בֶּן דָּוִד.

Eiliyahu hanavi, Eiliyahu haTishbi, Eiliyahu haGil'adi, bimheira yavo eileinu im mashi'ach ben David.

May Elijah the prophet, Elijah the Tishbite, Elijah of Gilead, arrive quickly together with the Messiah, son of David.

Recite the following:

שְׁפֹךְ חֲמָתְךָ אֶל הַגּוֹיִם אֲשֶׁר לֹא יְדָעוּךָ, וְעַל מַמְלָכוֹת אֲשֶׁר בְּשִׁמְךָ לֹא קָרָאוּ. כִּי אָכַל אֶת יַעֲקֹב וְאֶת נָוֵהוּ הֵשַׁמּוּ. שְׁפָךְ עֲלֵיהֶם זַעְמֶךָ, וַחֲרוֹן אַפְּךָ יַשִּׂיגֵם. תִּרְדֹּף בְּאַף וְתַשְׁמִידֵם מִתַּחַת שְׁמֵי יְהֹוָה.

Sh'fokh chamat'kha el hagoyim asher lo y'da'ukha, v'al mamlakhot asher b'shimkha lo kara'u. Hi akhal et Ya'akov v'et naveihu heishamu. Sh'fokh aleihem za'amekha, vacharon ap'kha yasigeim. Tirdof b'af v'tashmideim mitachat sh'mei Adonai.

Pour Your wrath upon the nations that do not recognize You and upon the kingdoms that do not invoke Your name. For they have consumed Jacob and laid waste to his habitation. Pour out Your fury upon them and let your burning anger overtake them. Pursue them with anger and annihilate them from under the skies of *HaShem*.

But Who Was He, Really?

If you imagine the prophet as a kindly old man with a soft white beard, the Bible has some jarring surprises in store. The historical Elijah was a fiery prophet best known for slaughtering hundreds of pagans on Mount Carmel—a tough-talking, hard-charging man of God who so irked the king that he had to flee into the desert and hide. There, on Mount Sinai, God speaks to him and asks him why the long face. Elijah, never one to mince words, declares that he feels lonely, presumably because he has despaired of his people and their all-too-human inclination to fall short of holiness. As one legend has it, God, punishing the prophet for his arrogance, commands him to visit every Seder in perpetuity, so that he may see that Jews still observe the old traditions and that there's hope for us all yet.

—*Liel Leibovitz*

Let Anne Roiphe take you on a walk with Elijah, master of sacrifice (page 134).

Hallel

A vestige from the days of the Temple, this prayer was said alongside the sacrifice of animals. (If you love your pet, sing a little louder.)

לֹא לָנוּ יְהוָה לֹא לָנוּ, כִּי לְשִׁמְךָ תֵּן כָּבוֹד עַל חַסְדְּךָ עַל אֲמִתֶּךָ. לָמָּה יֹאמְרוּ הַגּוֹיִם אַיֵּה נָא אֱלֹהֵיהֶם. וֵאלֹהֵינוּ בַשָּׁמָיִם כֹּל אֲשֶׁר חָפֵץ עָשָׂה. עֲצַבֵּיהֶם כֶּסֶף וְזָהָב, מַעֲשֵׂה יְדֵי אָדָם. פֶּה לָהֶם וְלֹא יְדַבֵּרוּ, עֵינַיִם לָהֶם וְלֹא יִרְאוּ. אָזְנַיִם לָהֶם וְלֹא יִשְׁמָעוּ, אַף לָהֶם וְלֹא יְרִיחוּן. יְדֵיהֶם וְלֹא יְמִישׁוּן, רַגְלֵיהֶם וְלֹא יְהַלֵּכוּ, לֹא יֶהְגּוּ בִּגְרוֹנָם. כְּמוֹהֶם יִהְיוּ עֹשֵׂיהֶם כֹּל אֲשֶׁר בֹּטֵחַ בָּהֶם. יִשְׂרָאֵל בְּטַח בַּיהוָה, עֶזְרָם וּמָגִנָּם הוּא. בֵּית אַהֲרֹן בִּטְחוּ בַּיהוָה, עֶזְרָם וּמָגִנָּם הוּא. יִרְאֵי יְהוָה בִּטְחוּ בַּיהוָה, עֶזְרָם וּמָגִנָּם הוּא.

Lo lanu Adonai lo lanu, ki l'shimkha tein kavod al chasd'kha al amitekha. Lama yom'ru hagoyim ayei na eloheihem. vEiloheinu vashamayim kol asher chafeitz asa. Atzabeihem kesef v'zahav ma'asei y'dei adam. Pe lahem v'lo y'dabeiru, einayim lahem v'lo yir'u. Oznayim lahem v'lo yishma'u, af lahem v'lo y'richun. Y'deihem v'lo y'mishun, ragleihem v'lo y'haleikhu, lo yehgu bigronam. K'mohem yihyu oseihem, kol asher bote'ach bahem. Yisra'eil batach bAdonai, ezram umaginam hu. Beit Aharon bitchu bAdonai, ezram umaginam hu. Yir'ei Adonai bitchu bAdonai, ezram umaginam hu.

Not for our sake, *HaShem*, not for our sake but for the sake of Your name bring glory, for Your kindness and Your faithfulness. Why should the nations say, "Where is their God now?" when our God is in heaven, doing as He pleases. Their idols are silver and gold, man's handiwork. They have mouths but cannot speak; eyes but cannot see; ears but cannot hear; noses but cannot smell; hands but cannot touch; feet but

What's something you could sacrifice this year? And why?

cannot walk; they can utter no sound from their throats. Those who fashion them—all who believe in them—should become like them. Israel, trust in the Lord! He is their help and shield. House of Aaron, trust in the Lord! He is their help and shield. You who fear the Lord, trust in the Lord! He is their help and shield.

יְהֹוָה זְכָרָנוּ יְבָרֵךְ, יְבָרֵךְ אֶת בֵּית יִשְׂרָאֵל, יְבָרֵךְ אֶת בֵּית אַהֲרֹן. יְבָרֵךְ יִרְאֵי יְהֹוָה, הַקְּטַנִּים עִם הַגְּדֹלִים. יֹסֵף יְהֹוָה עֲלֵיכֶם, עֲלֵיכֶם וְעַל בְּנֵיכֶם. בְּרוּכִים אַתֶּם לַיהֹוָה, עֹשֵׂה שָׁמַיִם וָאָרֶץ. הַשָּׁמַיִם, שָׁמַיִם לַיהֹוָה, וְהָאָרֶץ נָתַן לִבְנֵי אָדָם. לֹא הַמֵּתִים יְהַלְלוּ יָהּ, וְלֹא כָּל יֹרְדֵי דוּמָה. וַאֲנַחְנוּ נְבָרֵךְ יָהּ, מֵעַתָּה וְעַד עוֹלָם הַלְלוּיָהּ.

Adonai z'kharanu y'vareikh, y'vareikh et beit Yisra'eil, y'vareikh et beit Aharon. Y'vareikh yir'ei Adonai, hak'tanim im hag'dolim. Yoseif Adonai aleikhem, aleikhem v'al b'neikhem. B'rukhim atem lAdonai, ose shamayim va'aretz. Hashamayim, shamayim lAdonai, v'ha'aretz natan livnei adam. Lo hameitim y'hal'lu Yah, v'lo kol yor'dei duma. Va'anachnu n'vareikh Yah, mei'ata v'ad olam Hal'luyah.

HaShem who is mindful of us will bless—He will bless the House of Israel, He will bless the house of Aaron, He will bless those who fear *HaShem*, small and great alike. May *HaShem* increase your numbers, both yours and your children's. You are blessed by *HaShem*, Maker of heaven and earth. As for the heavens, they belong to *HaShem*, but the earth He gave to man. The dead cannot praise *HaShem*, nor any who descend into silence, but we will bless *HaShem* now and forever. Hallelujah!

אָהַבְתִּי כִּי יִשְׁמַע יְהֹוָה אֶת קוֹלִי תַּחֲנוּנָי. כִּי הִטָּה אָזְנוֹ לִי וּבְיָמַי אֶקְרָא. אֲפָפוּנִי חֶבְלֵי מָוֶת וּמְצָרֵי שְׁאוֹל מְצָאוּנִי, צָרָה וְיָגוֹן אֶמְצָא. וּבְשֵׁם יְהֹוָה אֶקְרָא, אָנָּה יְהֹוָה מַלְּטָה נַפְשִׁי. חַנּוּן יְהֹוָה וְצַדִּיק וֵאלֹהֵינוּ מְרַחֵם. שֹׁמֵר פְּתָאִים יְהֹוָה, דַּלּוֹתִי וְלִי יְהוֹשִׁיעַ. שׁוּבִי נַפְשִׁי לִמְנוּחָיְכִי כִּי יְהֹוָה גָּמַל עָלָיְכִי. כִּי חִלַּצְתָּ נַפְשִׁי מִמָּוֶת, אֶת עֵינִי מִן דִּמְעָה, אֶת רַגְלִי מִדֶּחִי. אֶתְהַלֵּךְ לִפְנֵי יְהֹוָה בְּאַרְצוֹת הַחַיִּים. הֶאֱמַנְתִּי כִּי אֲדַבֵּר, אֲנִי עָנִיתִי מְאֹד. אֲנִי אָמַרְתִּי בְחָפְזִי כָּל הָאָדָם כֹּזֵב.

Ahavti ki yishma Adonai et koli tachanunai. Ki hita ozno li uvyamai ekra. Afafuni chevlei mavet umtzarei Sh'ol m'tza'uni, tzara v'yagon emtza. Uvsheim Adonai ekra, ana Adonai mal'ta nafshi. Chanun Adonai v'tzadik, vEiloheinu m'racheim. Shomeir p'ta'im Adonai, daloti v'li y'hoshi'a. Shuvi nafshi limnuchay'khi ki Adonai gamal alay'khi. Ki chilatza nafshi mimavet, et eini min dim'a, et ragli midechi. Et-halekh lifnei Adonai b'artzot hachayim. He'emanti ki adabeir, ani aniti m'od. Ani amarti v'chofzi kol ha'adam kozeiv.

I love *HaShem* for He hears my voice, my pleas; He listens whenever I call out. The bonds of death encircled me, the confines of the grave found me—I came upon trouble and sorrow. So I invoked *HaShem*'s name: "*HaShem*, save my life!" *HaShem* is gracious and righteous; God is merciful. *HaShem* protects the simple; I was cut down and He saved me. Be at rest, once again, my soul, for *HaShem* has been kind to you. You have delivered me from death, my eyes from tears, my feet from stumbling. I will walk before *HaShem* in the lands of the living. I have kept faith although in my great suffering I spoke rashly, saying, "all mankind is deceitful."

מָה אָשִׁיב לַיהוָה כָּל תַּגְמוּלוֹהִי עָלָי. כּוֹס
יְשׁוּעוֹת אֶשָּׂא וּבְשֵׁם יְהוָה אֶקְרָא. נְדָרַי
לַיהוָה אֲשַׁלֵּם נֶגְדָה נָּא לְכָל עַמּוֹ. יָקָר
בְּעֵינֵי יְהוָה הַמָּוְתָה לַחֲסִידָיו. אָנָּה יְהוָה כִּי
אֲנִי עַבְדֶּךָ, אֲנִי עַבְדְּךָ בֶּן אֲמָתֶךָ, פִּתַּחְתָּ
לְמוֹסֵרָי. לְךָ אֶזְבַּח זֶבַח תּוֹדָה וּבְשֵׁם יְהוָה
אֶקְרָא. נְדָרַי לַיהוָה אֲשַׁלֵּם נֶגְדָה נָּא לְכָל
עַמּוֹ. בְּחַצְרוֹת בֵּית יְהוָה, בְּתוֹכֵכִי יְרוּשָׁלָיִם,
הַלְלוּיָהּ.

Ma ashiv lAdonai kol tagmulohi alai. Kos y'shu'ot esa uvsheim Adonai ekra. N'darai lAdonai ashaleim negda na l'khol amo. Yakar b'einei Adonai hamav'ta lachasidav. Ana Adonai ki ani avdekha, ani avd'kha ben amatekha, pitachta l'moseirai. L'kha ezbach zevach toda uvsheim Adonai ekra. N'darai lAdonai ashaleim negda na l'khol amo. B'chatzrot beit Adonai, b'tokheikhi Y'rushalayim, Hal'luyah.

How can I repay *HaShem* for all His kindness to me? I will raise the cup of deliverance and invoke *HaShem*'s name. I will pay my vows to *HaShem*, in the presence of His entire people. The death of His devout ones is grievous in *HaShem*'s eyes. Please *HaShem*, I am Your servant, Your servant the son of Your maidservant—You have released my bonds. I will sacrifice a thanksgiving offering to You and invoke *HaShem*'s name. I will pay my vows to *HaShem*, in the presence of His entire people, in the courtyards of the house of *HaShem*, in the midst of Jerusalem. Hallelujah!

LEAPFROG

The next big moment is the Fourth Cup (page 109).

הַלְלוּ אֶת יְהֹוָה כָּל גּוֹיִם, שַׁבְּחוּהוּ כָּל הָאֻמִּים.
כִּי גָבַר עָלֵינוּ חַסְדּוֹ, וֶאֱמֶת יְהֹוָה לְעוֹלָם,
הַלְלוּיָהּ.

Hal'lu et Adonai kol goyim, shab'chuhu
kol ha'umim. Ki gavar aleinu chasdo
ve'emet Adonai l'olam, Hal'luyah.

Praise *HaShem*, all you nations; extol Him all you peoples. For His kindness
has overwhelmed us and *HaShem*'s faithfulness is forever. Hallelujah!

הוֹדוּ לַיהֹוָה כִּי טוֹב,
כִּי לְעוֹלָם חַסְדּוֹ.

Hodu lAdonai ki tov,
ki l'olam chasdo.

יֹאמַר נָא יִשְׂרָאֵל,
כִּי לְעוֹלָם חַסְדּוֹ.

Yomar na Yisra'eil,
ki l'olam chasdo.

יֹאמְרוּ נָא בֵית אַהֲרֹן,
כִּי לְעוֹלָם חַסְדּוֹ.

Yom'ru na veit Aharon,
ki l'olam chasdo.

יֹאמְרוּ נָא יִרְאֵי יְהֹוָה,
כִּי לְעוֹלָם חַסְדּוֹ.

Yom'ru na yir'ei Adonai,
ki l'olam chasdo.

Thank *HaShem*, since He is good, His kindness endures forever.
Let Israel now say, "His kindness endures forever."
Let the House of Aaron now say, "His kindness endures forever."
Let those who fear *HaShem* now say, "His kindness endures forever."

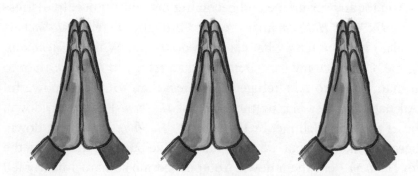

מִן הַמֵּצַר קָרָאתִי יָּהּ, עָנָנִי בַמֶּרְחָב יָהּ. יְהֹוָה לִי לֹא אִירָא, מַה יַּעֲשֶׂה לִי אָדָם. יְהֹוָה לִי בְּעֹזְרָי וַאֲנִי אֶרְאֶה בְשֹׂנְאָי. טוֹב לַחֲסוֹת בַּיהֹוָה מִבְּטֹחַ בָּאָדָם. טוֹב לַחֲסוֹת בַּיהֹוָה מִבְּטֹחַ בִּנְדִיבִים. כָּל גּוֹיִם סְבָבוּנִי בְּשֵׁם יְהֹוָה כִּי אֲמִילַם. סַבּוּנִי גַם סְבָבוּנִי בְּשֵׁם יְהֹוָה כִּי אֲמִילַם. סַבּוּנִי כִדְבוֹרִים, דֹּעֲכוּ כְּאֵשׁ קוֹצִים בְּשֵׁם יְהֹוָה כִּי אֲמִילַם. דָּחֹה דְחִיתַנִי לִנְפֹּל וַיהֹוָה עֲזָרָנִי. עָזִּי וְזִמְרָת יָהּ וַיְהִי לִי לִישׁוּעָה. קוֹל רִנָּה וִישׁוּעָה בְּאָהֳלֵי צַדִּיקִים, יְמִין יְהֹוָה עֹשָׂה חָיִל. יְמִין יְהֹוָה רוֹמֵמָה, יְמִין יְהֹוָה עֹשָׂה חָיִל. לֹא אָמוּת כִּי אֶחְיֶה וַאֲסַפֵּר מַעֲשֵׂי יָהּ. יַסֹּר יִסְּרַנִּי יָּהּ וְלַמָּוֶת לֹא נְתָנָנִי. פִּתְחוּ לִי שַׁעֲרֵי צֶדֶק, אָבֹא בָם אוֹדֶה יָהּ. זֶה הַשַּׁעַר לַיהֹוָה, צַדִּיקִים יָבֹאוּ בוֹ.

אוֹדְךָ כִּי עֲנִיתָנִי וַתְּהִי לִי לִישׁוּעָה. אוֹדְךָ כִּי עֲנִיתָנִי וַתְּהִי לִי לִישׁוּעָה. אֶבֶן מָאֲסוּ הַבּוֹנִים הָיְתָה לְרֹאשׁ פִּנָּה. אֶבֶן מָאֲסוּ הַבּוֹנִים הָיְתָה לְרֹאשׁ פִּנָּה. מֵאֵת יְהֹוָה הָיְתָה זֹּאת, הִיא נִפְלָאת בְּעֵינֵינוּ. מֵאֵת יְהֹוָה הָיְתָה זֹּאת, הִיא נִפְלָאת בְּעֵינֵינוּ. זֶה הַיּוֹם עָשָׂה יְהֹוָה נָגִילָה וְנִשְׂמְחָה בוֹ. זֶה הַיּוֹם עָשָׂה יְהֹוָה נָגִילָה וְנִשְׂמְחָה בוֹ.

Min hameitzar karati Yah, anani vamerchav Yah. Adonai li lo ira, ma ya'ase li adam. Adonai li b'oz'rai, va'ani er'e v'son'ai. Tov lachasot bAdonai, mib'to'ach ba'adam. Tov lachasot bAdonai, mib'to'ach bindivim. Kol goyim s'vavuni, b'sheim Adonai ki amilam. Sabuni gam s'vavuni, b'sheim Adonai ki amilam. Sabuni khidvorim, do'akhu k'eish kotzim b'sheim Adonai ki amilam. Dakho d'khitani linpol, vAdonai azarani. Ozi v'zimrat Yah, vayhi li lishu'a. Kol rina vishu'a b'oholei tzadikim, y'min Adonai osa chayil. Y'min Adonai romeima, y'min Adonai osa chayil. Lo amut ki echye va'asapeir ma'asei Yah. Yasor yis'rani Yah v'lamavet lo n'tanani. Pitchu li sha'arei tzedek, avo vam ode Yah. Ze hasha'ar lAdonai, tzadikim yavo'u vo.

Od'kha ki anitani vat'hi li lishu'a. Od'kha ki anitani vat'hi li lishu'a. Even ma'asu habonim hay'ta l'rosh pina. Even ma'asu habonim hay'ta l'rosh pina. Mei'eit Adonai hay'ta zot, hi niflat b'eineinu. Mei'eit Adonai hay'ta zot, hi niflat b'eineinu. Ze hayom asa Adonai nagila v'nism'cha vo. Ze hayom asa Adonai nagila v'nism'cha vo.

I thank You for answering me and becoming my deliverance. In distress I called on *HaShem*; *HaShem* answered and brought me relief. *HaShem* is on my side, I have no fear; what can man do to me? With *HaShem* supporting me, I can face my foes. Better to take refuge in *HaShem* than to rely on man; better to take refuge in *HaShem* than to rely on powerful men. All nations beset me; by the name of *HaShem* I cut them down. They beset and encircled me, by the name of *HaShem* I cut them down. They beset me like bees but are extinguished like burning thorns; by the name of *HaShem* I cut them down. You pushed me so hard I nearly fell but *HaShem* helped me. *HaShem* is my might and praise, He has become my deliverance. Jubilation due to deliverance resounds in the tents of the righteous: "*HaShem*'s right hand is triumphant! *HaShem*'s right hand is raised high, *HaShem*'s right hand is triumphant!" I will not die but will live to relate *HaShem*'s deeds. *HaShem* chastened me severely, but did not let me die. Open the gates of righteousness for me that I may enter them and thank *HaShem*. This is the gateway to *HaShem*, the righteous will enter through it.

I thank You for answering me and becoming my deliverance. The stone that the builders rejected has become the cornerstone. The stone that the builders rejected has become the cornerstone. This is *HaShem*'s doing; it is marvelous in our eyes. This is *HaShem*'s doing; it is marvelous in our eyes. This is the day that *HaShem* has made—let us rejoice and be glad on it! This is the day that *HaShem* has made—let us rejoice and be glad on it!

אָנָּא יְהֹוָה הוֹשִׁיעָה נָּא.

Ana Adonai hoshi'a na.

אָנָּא יְהֹוָה הוֹשִׁיעָה נָּא.

Ana Adonai hoshi'a na.

אָנָּא יְהֹוָה הַצְלִיחָה נָּא.

Ana Adonai hatzlicha na.

אָנָּא יְהֹוָה הַצְלִיחָה נָּא.

Ana Adonai hatzlicha na.

Please, *HaShem*, bring salvation now; please, *HaShem*, bring salvation now! Please, *HaShem*, bring prosperity now; please, *HaShem*, bring prosperity now!

RELIEF

בָּרוּךְ הַבָּא בְּשֵׁם יְהֹוָה, בֵּרַכְנוּכֶם מִבֵּית יְהֹוָה. בָּרוּךְ הַבָּא בְּשֵׁם יְהֹוָה, בֵּרַכְנוּכֶם מִבֵּית יְהֹוָה.

Barukh haba b'sheim Adonai, beirakhnukhem mibeit Adonai. Barukh haba b'sheim Adonai, beirakhnukhem mibeit Adonai.

אֵל יְהֹוָה וַיָּאֶר לָנוּ, אִסְרוּ חַג בַּעֲבֹתִים עַד קַרְנוֹת הַמִּזְבֵּחַ. אֵל יְהֹוָה וַיָּאֶר לָנוּ, אִסְרוּ חַג בַּעֲבֹתִים עַד קַרְנוֹת הַמִּזְבֵּחַ.

Eil Adonai vaya'er lanu, isru chag ba'avotim ad karnot hamizbe'ach. Eil Adonai vaya'er lanu, isru chag ba'avotim ad karnot hamizbe'ach.

אֵלִי אַתָּה וְאוֹדֶךָּ, אֱלֹהַי אֲרוֹמְמֶךָּ. אֵלִי אַתָּה וְאוֹדֶךָּ, אֱלֹהַי אֲרוֹמְמֶךָּ.

Eili ata v'odeka, Elohai arom'meka. Eili ata v'odeka, Elohai arom'meka.

הוֹדוּ לַיהֹוָה כִּי טוֹב, כִּי לְעוֹלָם חַסְדּוֹ. הוֹדוּ לַיהֹוָה כִּי טוֹב, כִּי לְעוֹלָם חַסְדּוֹ.

Hodu lAdonai ki tov, ki l'olam chasdo. Hodu lAdonai ki tov, ki l'olam chasdo.

Blessed are those who come in *HaShem*'s name; we bless you from *HaShem*'s house. Blessed are those who come in *HaShem*'s name; we bless you from *HaShem*'s house.

HaShem is God; He has given us light; bind the festival offering to the altar's horns with cords. *HaShem* is God; He has given us light; bind the festival offering to the altar's horns with cords. You are my God and I will thank You; You are my God and I will exalt You. You are my God and I will thank You; You are my God and I will exalt You. Thank *HaShem*, since He is good, His kindness endures forever. Thank *HaShem*, since He is good, His kindness endures forever.

יְהַלְלוּךְ יְהוָה אֱלֹהֵינוּ כָּל מַעֲשֶׂיךָ, וַחֲסִידֶיךָ
צַדִּיקִים עוֹשֵׂי רְצוֹנֶךָ, וְכָל עַמְּךָ בֵּית יִשְׂרָאֵל,
בְּרִנָּה יוֹדוּ וִיבָרְכוּ וִישַׁבְּחוּ וִיפָאֲרוּ וִישׁוֹרְרוּ
וִירוֹמְמוּ וְיַעֲרִיצוּ וְיַקְדִּישׁוּ וְיַמְלִיכוּ אֶת שִׁמְךָ
מַלְכֵּנוּ. כִּי לְךָ טוֹב לְהוֹדוֹת וּלְשִׁמְךָ נָאֶה
לְזַמֵּר, כִּי מֵעוֹלָם וְעַד עוֹלָם אַתָּה אֵל.

Y'hal'lukha Adonai Eloheinu kol ma'asekha, vachasidekha tzadikim osei r'tzonekha, v'khol am'kha beit Yisra'eil, b'rina yodu vivar'khu vishab'khu vifa'aru virom'mu v'ya'aritzu v'yakdishu v'yamlikhu et shimkha malkeinu. Ki l'kha tov l'hodot ulshimkha na'e l'zameir, ki mei'olam v'ad olam ata Eil.

All your works will praise You, *HaShem*, our God. Your devoutly righteous ones who do Your will, and all the people of the House of Israel will joyously thank, bless, laud, glorify, praise, exalt, extol, sanctify, and proclaim the sovereignty of Your name, our Ruler, at all times. For it is fitting to thank You and proper to sing the praises of Your name, for You are God forever and ever.

הוֹדוּ לַיהוָה כִּי טוֹב,
כִּי לְעוֹלָם חַסְדּוֹ.

Hodu lAdonai ki tov,
ki l'olam chasdo.

הוֹדוּ לֵאלֹהֵי הָאֱלֹהִים,
כִּי לְעוֹלָם חַסְדּוֹ.

Hodu lEilohei ha'Elohim,
ki l'olam chasdo.

הוֹדוּ לַאֲדֹנֵי הָאֲדֹנִים,
כִּי לְעוֹלָם חַסְדּוֹ.

Hodu lAdonei ha'adonim,
ki l'olam chasdo.

לְעֹשֵׂה נִפְלָאוֹת גְּדֹלוֹת לְבַדּוֹ,
כִּי לְעוֹלָם חַסְדּוֹ.

L'osei nifla'ot g'dolot l'vado,
ki l'olam chasdo.

לְעֹשֵׂה הַשָּׁמַיִם בִּתְבוּנָה,
כִּי לְעוֹלָם חַסְדּוֹ.

L'osei hashamayim bitvuna,
ki l'olam chasdo.

לְרֹקַע הָאָרֶץ עַל הַמָּיִם,
כִּי לְעוֹלָם חַסְדּוֹ.

L'roka ha'aretz al hamayim,
ki l'olam chasdo.

<table>
<tr><td>לְעֹשֵׂה אוֹרִים גְּדֹלִים,
כִּי לְעוֹלָם חַסְדּוֹ.</td><td>L'osei orim g'dolim,
ki l'olam chasdo.</td></tr>
<tr><td>אֶת הַשֶּׁמֶשׁ לְמֶמְשֶׁלֶת בַּיּוֹם,
כִּי לְעוֹלָם חַסְדּוֹ.</td><td>Et hashemesh l'memshelet bayom,
ki l'olam chasdo.</td></tr>
<tr><td>אֶת הַיָּרֵחַ וְכוֹכָבִים לְמֶמְשְׁלוֹת בַּלָּיְלָה,
כִּי לְעוֹלָם חַסְדּוֹ.</td><td>Et hayare'ach v'khokhavim
l'memsh'lot balaila,
ki l'olam chasdo.</td></tr>
<tr><td>לְמַכֵּה מִצְרַיִם בִּבְכוֹרֵיהֶם,
כִּי לְעוֹלָם חַסְדּוֹ.</td><td>L'makei Mitzrayim bivkhoreihem,
ki l'olam chasdo.</td></tr>
<tr><td>וַיּוֹצֵא יִשְׂרָאֵל מִתּוֹכָם,
כִּי לְעוֹלָם חַסְדּוֹ.</td><td>Vayotzei Yisra'eil mitokham,
ki l'olam chasdo.</td></tr>
<tr><td>בְּיָד חֲזָקָה וּבִזְרוֹעַ נְטוּיָה,
כִּי לְעוֹלָם חַסְדּוֹ.</td><td>B'yad chazaka uvizro'a n'tuya,
ki l'olam chasdo.</td></tr>
<tr><td>לְגֹזֵר יַם סוּף לִגְזָרִים,
כִּי לְעוֹלָם חַסְדּוֹ.</td><td>L'gozeir Yam Suf ligzarim,
ki l'olam chasdo.</td></tr>
<tr><td>וְהֶעֱבִיר יִשְׂרָאֵל בְּתוֹכוֹ,
כִּי לְעוֹלָם חַסְדּוֹ.</td><td>V'he'evir Yisra'eil b'tokho,
ki l'olam chasdo.</td></tr>
<tr><td>וְנִעֵר פַּרְעֹה וְחֵילוֹ בְיַם סוּף,
כִּי לְעוֹלָם חַסְדּוֹ.</td><td>V'ni'eir Par'o v'cheilo v'Yam Suf,
ki l'olam chasdo.</td></tr>
<tr><td>לְמוֹלִיךְ עַמּוֹ בַּמִּדְבָּר,
כִּי לְעוֹלָם חַסְדּוֹ.</td><td>L'molikh amo bamidbar,
ki l'olam chasdo.</td></tr>
<tr><td>לְמַכֵּה מְלָכִים גְּדֹלִים,
כִּי לְעוֹלָם חַסְדּוֹ.</td><td>L'makei m'lakhim g'dolim,
ki l'olam chasdo.</td></tr>
<tr><td>וַיַּהֲרֹג מְלָכִים אַדִּירִים,
כִּי לְעוֹלָם חַסְדּוֹ.</td><td>Vayaharog m'lakhim adirim,
ki l'olam chasdo.</td></tr>
<tr><td>לְסִיחוֹן מֶלֶךְ הָאֱמֹרִי,
כִּי לְעוֹלָם חַסְדּוֹ.</td><td>L'Sichon melekh ha'Emori,
ki l'olam chasdo.</td></tr>
<tr><td>וּלְעוֹג מֶלֶךְ הַבָּשָׁן,
כִּי לְעוֹלָם חַסְדּוֹ.</td><td>UlOg melekh haBashan,
ki l'olam chasdo.</td></tr>
</table>

FOREVER

& EVER

& EVER

& EVER

וְנָתַן אַרְצָם לְנַחֲלָה,
כִּי לְעוֹלָם חַסְדּוֹ.

V'natan artzam l'nachala,
ki l'olam chasdo.

נַחֲלָה לְיִשְׂרָאֵל עַבְדּוֹ,
כִּי לְעוֹלָם חַסְדּוֹ.

Nachala l'Yisra'eil avdo,
ki l'olam chasdo.

שֶׁבְּשִׁפְלֵנוּ זָכַר לָנוּ,
כִּי לְעוֹלָם חַסְדּוֹ.

Sheb'shifleinu zakhar lanu,
ki l'olam chasdo.

וַיִּפְרְקֵנוּ מִצָּרֵינוּ,
כִּי לְעוֹלָם חַסְדּוֹ.

Vayifr'keinu mitzareinu,
ki l'olam chasdo.

נֹתֵן לֶחֶם לְכָל בָּשָׂר,
כִּי לְעוֹלָם חַסְדּוֹ.

Notein lekhem l'khol basar,
ki l'olam chasdo.

הוֹדוּ לְאֵל הַשָּׁמָיִם,
כִּי לְעוֹלָם חַסְדּוֹ.

Hodu l'Eil hashamayim,
ki l'olam chasdo.

Thank *HaShem*, for He is good,
His kindness endures forever.

Thank the supreme God,
His kindness endures forever.

Thank the Lord of lords,
His kindness endures forever.

Who alone performs great marvels,
His kindness endures forever.

Who made the heavens with wisdom,
His kindness endures forever.

Who spread out the earth over the waters,
His kindness endures forever.

Who made the great lights,
His kindness endures forever.

The sun to rule during the day,
His kindness endures forever.

The moon and stars to rule during the night,
His kindness endures forever.

Who struck down the Egyptian firstborn,
His kindness endures forever.

And brought out Israel from their midst,
His kindness endures forever.

With a mighty hand and an outstretched arm,
His kindness endures forever.

Who split the Sea of Reeds,
His kindness endures forever.

And took Israel through it,
His kindness endures forever.

KINDNESS

And cast Pharaoh and his army into the Sea,
His kindness endures forever.

Who led His people through the wilderness,
His kindness endures forever.

Who struck down great kings,
His kindness endures forever.

ENDURES

And killed mighty rulers,
His kindness endures forever.

Sichon, king of the Emorites,
His kindness endures forever.

And Og, king of Bashan,
His kindness endures forever.

And gave their land as a heritage,
His kindness endures forever.

FOREVER

A heritage for His servant Israel,
His kindness endures forever.

Who in our lowliness remembered us,
His kindness endures forever.

And saved us from our enemies,
His kindness endures forever.

Who gives nourishment to all flesh,
His kindness endures forever.

Thank God in heaven,
His kindness endures forever.

נִשְׁמַת כָּל חַי תְּבָרֵךְ אֶת שִׁמְךָ, יְהֹוָה אֱלֹהֵינוּ, וְרוּחַ כָּל בָּשָׂר תְּפָאֵר וּתְרוֹמֵם זִכְרְךָ מַלְכֵּנוּ תָּמִיד. מִן הָעוֹלָם וְעַד הָעוֹלָם אַתָּה אֵל, וּמִבַּלְעָדֶיךָ אֵין לָנוּ מֶלֶךְ גּוֹאֵל וּמוֹשִׁיעַ, פּוֹדֶה וּמַצִּיל וּמְפַרְנֵס וּמְרַחֵם בְּכָל עֵת צָרָה וְצוּקָה. אֵין לָנוּ מֶלֶךְ אֶלָּא אָתָּה. אֱלֹהֵי הָרִאשׁוֹנִים וְהָאַחֲרוֹנִים, אֱלוֹהַּ כָּל בְּרִיּוֹת, אֲדוֹן כָּל תּוֹלָדוֹת, הַמְהֻלָּל בְּרֹב הַתִּשְׁבָּחוֹת, הַמְנַהֵג עוֹלָמוֹ בְּחֶסֶד וּבְרִיּוֹתָיו בְּרַחֲמִים. וַיהֹוָה לֹא יָנוּם וְלֹא יִישָׁן. הַמְעוֹרֵר יְשֵׁנִים וְהַמֵּקִיץ נִרְדָּמִים, וְהַמֵּשִׂיחַ אִלְּמִים וְהַמַּתִּיר אֲסוּרִים, וְהַסּוֹמֵךְ נוֹפְלִים וְהַזּוֹקֵף כְּפוּפִים, לְךָ לְבַדְּךָ אֲנַחְנוּ מוֹדִים. אִלּוּ פִינוּ מָלֵא שִׁירָה כַּיָּם, וּלְשׁוֹנֵנוּ רִנָּה כַּהֲמוֹן גַּלָּיו, וְשִׂפְתוֹתֵינוּ שֶׁבַח כְּמֶרְחֲבֵי רָקִיעַ, וְעֵינֵינוּ מְאִירוֹת כַּשֶּׁמֶשׁ וְכַיָּרֵחַ, וְיָדֵינוּ פְרוּשׂוֹת כְּנִשְׁרֵי שָׁמָיִם, וְרַגְלֵינוּ קַלּוֹת כָּאַיָּלוֹת, אֵין אֲנַחְנוּ מַסְפִּיקִים לְהוֹדוֹת לְךָ, יְהֹוָה אֱלֹהֵינוּ וֵאלֹהֵי אֲבוֹתֵינוּ, וּלְבָרֵךְ אֶת שִׁמְךָ עַל אַחַת מֵאֶלֶף אֶלֶף אַלְפֵי אֲלָפִים וְרִבֵּי רְבָבוֹת פְּעָמִים הַטּוֹבוֹת שֶׁעָשִׂיתָ עִם אֲבוֹתֵינוּ וְעִמָּנוּ. מִמִּצְרַיִם גְּאַלְתָּנוּ, יְהֹוָה אֱלֹהֵינוּ, וּמִבֵּית עֲבָדִים פְּדִיתָנוּ, בְּרָעָב זַנְתָּנוּ וּבְשָׂבָע כִּלְכַּלְתָּנוּ, מֵחֶרֶב הִצַּלְתָּנוּ וּמִדֶּבֶר מִלַּטְתָּנוּ, וּמֵחֳלָיִם רָעִים וְנֶאֱמָנִים דִּלִּיתָנוּ. עַד הֵנָּה עֲזָרוּנוּ רַחֲמֶיךָ וְלֹא עֲזָבוּנוּ חֲסָדֶיךָ וְאַל תִּטְּשֵׁנוּ יְהֹוָה אֱלֹהֵינוּ לָנֶצַח. עַל כֵּן אֵבָרִים שֶׁפִּלַּגְתָּ בָּנוּ וְרוּחַ וּנְשָׁמָה שֶׁנָּפַחְתָּ בְּאַפֵּינוּ וְלָשׁוֹן אֲשֶׁר שַׂמְתָּ בְּפִינוּ, הֵן הֵם יוֹדוּ וִיבָרְכוּ וִישַׁבְּחוּ וִיפָאֲרוּ וִירוֹמְמוּ וְיַעֲרִיצוּ וְיַקְדִּישׁוּ וְיַמְלִיכוּ אֶת שִׁמְךָ מַלְכֵּנוּ. כִּי כָל פֶּה לְךָ יוֹדֶה, וְכָל לָשׁוֹן לְךָ תִשָּׁבַע, וְכָל בֶּרֶךְ לְךָ תִכְרַע, וְכָל קוֹמָה לְפָנֶיךָ תִשְׁתַּחֲוֶה, וְכָל לְבָבוֹת יִירָאוּךָ, וְכָל קֶרֶב וּכְלָיוֹת יְזַמְּרוּ לִשְׁמֶךָ, כַּדָּבָר שֶׁכָּתוּב: "כָּל עַצְמֹתַי תֹּאמַרְנָה יְהֹוָה מִי

Nishmat kol chai t'vareikh et shimkha, Adonai Eloheinu, v'ru'ach kol basar t'fa'eir utromeim zikhr'kha malkeinu tamid. Min ha'olam v'ad olam ata Eil, umibal'adekha ein lanu melekh go'eil umoshi'a, pode umatzil umfarneis umracheim b'khol eit tzara v'tzuka. Ein lanu melekh ela ata. Elohei harishonim v'ha'acharonim, Elo'ah kol b'riyot, adon kol toladot, ham'hulal b'rov hatishbachot, ham'naheig olamo b'chesed uvriyotav b'rachamim. VAdonai lo yanum v'lo yishan. Ham'oreir y'sheinim v'hameikitz nirdamim, v'hameisi'ach il'mim v'hamatir asurim, v'hasomeikh nof'lim v'hazokeif k'fufim, l'kha l'vad'kha anachnu modim. Ilu finu malei shira kayam, ulshoneinu rina kahamon galav, v'siftoteinu shevach k'merchavei raki'a, v'eineinu m'irot kashemesh v'khaye'ach, v'yadeinu f'rusot k'nishrei shamayim, v'ragleinu kalot ka'ayalot, ein anachnu maspikim l'hodot l'kha, Adonai Eloheinu vElohei avoteinu, ulvareikh et shimkha al achat mei'alef elef alfei alafim v'ribei r'vavot p'amim hatovot she'asita im avoteinu v'imanu. Mimitzrayim g'altanu, Adonai Eloheinu, umibeit avadim p'ditanu, b'ra'av zantanu uvsava kilkaltanu, mei'cherev hitzaltanu umidever milat'tanu, umeicholayim ra'im v'ne'emanim dilitanu. Ad heina azarunu rachamekha v'lo azavunu chasadekha v'al titsheinu Adonai Eloheinu lanetzach. Al kein eivarim shepilagta banu v'ru'ach unshama shenafachta v'apeinu v'lashon asher samta b'finu, hein heim yodu vivar'khu vishab'chu vifa'aru virom'mu v'ya'aritzu v'yakdishu v'yamlikhu et shimkha malkeinu. Ki khol pe l'kha yode, v'khol lashon l'kha tishava, v'khol berekh l'kha tikhra, v'khol koma l'fanekha tishtachave, v'khol l'vavot yira'ukha, v'khol kerev ukhlayot y'zam'ru lishmekha, kadavar shekatuv: "Kol atzmotai tomarna Adonai mi

כָמוֹךָ, מַצִּיל עָנִי מֵחָזָק מִמֶּנּוּ וְעָנִי וְאֶבְיוֹן מִגֹּזְלוֹ." מִי יִדְמֶה לָךְ וּמִי יִשְׁוֶה לָּךְ וּמִי יַעֲרָךְ לָךְ, הָאֵל הַגָּדוֹל הַגִּבּוֹר וְהַנּוֹרָא אֵל עֶלְיוֹן קֹנֵה שָׁמַיִם וָאָרֶץ. נְהַלֶּלְךָ וּנְשַׁבֵּחֲךָ וּנְפָאֶרְךָ וּנְבָרֵךְ אֶת שֵׁם קָדְשֶׁךָ, כָּאָמוּר: "לְדָוִד, בָּרְכִי נַפְשִׁי אֶת יְהוָה, וְכָל קְרָבַי אֶת שֵׁם קָדְשׁוֹ."

הָאֵל בְּתַעֲצֻמוֹת עֻזֶּךָ, הַגָּדוֹל בִּכְבוֹד שְׁמֶךָ, הַגִּבּוֹר לָנֶצַח וְהַנּוֹרָא בְּנוֹרְאוֹתֶיךָ, הַמֶּלֶךְ הַיּוֹשֵׁב עַל כִּסֵּא רָם וְנִשָּׂא. שׁוֹכֵן עַד מָרוֹם וְקָדוֹשׁ שְׁמוֹ. וְכָתוּב: "רַנְּנוּ צַדִּיקִים בַּיהוָה, לַיְשָׁרִים נָאוָה תְהִלָּה." בְּפִי יְשָׁרִים תִּתְהַלָּל, וּבְדִבְרֵי צַדִּיקִים תִּתְבָּרַךְ, וּבִלְשׁוֹן חֲסִידִים תִּתְרוֹמָם, וּבְקֶרֶב קְדוֹשִׁים תִּתְקַדָּשׁ. וּבְמַקְהֲלוֹת רִבְבוֹת עַמְּךָ בֵּית יִשְׂרָאֵל בְּרִנָּה יִתְפָּאַר שִׁמְךָ מַלְכֵּנוּ בְּכָל דּוֹר וָדוֹר. שֶׁכֵּן חוֹבַת כָּל הַיְצוּרִים לְפָנֶיךָ, יְהוָה אֱלֹהֵינוּ וֵאלֹהֵי אֲבוֹתֵינוּ, לְהוֹדוֹת לְהַלֵּל לְשַׁבֵּחַ לְפָאֵר לְרוֹמֵם לְהַדֵּר לְבָרֵךְ לְעַלֵּה וּלְקַלֵּס, עַל כָּל דִּבְרֵי שִׁירוֹת וְתִשְׁבְּחוֹת דָּוִד בֶּן יִשַׁי עַבְדְּךָ מְשִׁיחֶךָ.

khamokha, matzil ani meichazak mimenu v'ani v'evyon migoz'lo." Mi yidme lakh umi yishve lakh umi ya'arokh lakh, ha'Eil hagadol hagibor v'hanora Eil elyon kone shamayim va'aretz. N'halel'kha unshabeichakha unfa'erkha unvareikh et sheim kodshekha, ka'amur: "L'David, bar'khi nafshi et Adonai, v'khol k'ravai et sheim kodsho."

Ha'Eil b'ta'atzumot uzekha, hagadol bikhvod sh'mekha, hagibor lanetzach v'hanora b'nor'otekha, hamelekh hayosheiv al kisei ram v'nisa. Shokhein ad marom v'kadosh sh'mo. V'khatuv: "Ran'nu tzadikim bAdonai, laysharim nava t'hila." B'fi y'sharim tithalal, uvdivrei tzadikim litbarakh, uvilshon chasidim titromam, uvkerev k'doshim titkadash. Uvmakhalot riv'vot am'kha beit Yisra'eil b'rina yitpa'ar shimkha malkeinu b'khol dor vador. Shekein chovat kol haytzurim l'fanekha, Adonai Eloheinu vElohei avoteinu, l'hodot l'haleil l'shabe'ach l'fa'eir l'romeim l'hadeir l'vareikh l'alei ulkaleis, al kol divrei shirot v'tishb'chot David ben Yishai avd'kha m'shichekha.

The soul of every living thing blesses Your name, *HaShem*, our God, and the spirit of all flesh glorifies and exalts Your remembrance, our Ruler. From forever until forever You are God, and You are our only Ruler, Redeemer, and Savior. You are the One who liberates, rescues, sustains, and takes pity during every period of distress and anguish. We have no Ruler but You! God of the first and the last, God of all creatures, Master of all generations, praised with a multitude of praises, who governs His world with kindness and His creatures with mercy. *HaShem* neither sleeps nor slumbers. He rouses the sleepers and awakens the slumberers, makes the mute speak and releases the bound, supports the fallen and straightens the stooped. To You alone do we give thanks. Were our mouths as full of song as the sea, our tongue as full of paeans as its multitudinous waves, our lips as full of praise as the expanse of the skies, our eyes as brilliant as the sun and moon, our hands as outstretched as the vultures of the sky, our feet as swift as hinds—we still could not sufficiently thank You, *HaShem*, our God and God of our forefathers, and bless Your name for even one of the millions and billions of good deeds You have done for our forefathers and for us. *HaShem*, our God, You redeemed us from Egypt, rescued us from the house of bondage, sustained us in famine, sated us with plenty, saved us from the sword, let us escape plague, and spared us from terrible and enduring diseases. Your mercy has aided us until now and Your kindness has not left us—do not abandon us, *HaShem*, our God, ever! Therefore, let the organs that You set within us, the spirit and soul that You blew into our nostrils, and the tongue that You placed in our mouths, thank, bless, praise, glorify, exalt, extol, sanctify, and proclaim the sovereignty of Your name, our Ruler. For every mouth will thank You, every tongue vow allegiance to You, every knee bow to You, every spine prostrate itself to You, every heart fear You, and every fiber of my being sing praise to Your name. As it is written: "All my bones shall say, '*HaShem*, who is like You?' Who saves the poor from those of greater strength, the destitute from those who would rob him." Who is like You? Who equal to You? Who comparable to You? Great, mighty, awesome, supreme God, Creator of heaven and earth. We shall praise, exalt, glorify, and bless Your holy name, as it is said: "Of David: Bless *HaShem*, my soul, my entire being His holy name."

All-powerful in the force of Your strength, great in Your name's glory, eternally mighty and awesome in deed, the Ruler who sits on a high and lofty throne, who abides forever, exalted and holy in name. It is written: "Sing joyfully before *HaShem*, righteous ones, for praise befits the upright." By the mouth of the upright will You be lauded, by the words of the righteous will You be blessed, by the tongue of the pious will You be exalted, and among the holy will You be sanctified. In the assemblies of the myriads of Your people, the House of Israel, will Your name, our Ruler, be glorified in every generation with song. For such is the duty of all creatures to thank, praise, laud, glorify, exalt, honor, bless, elevate, and acclaim You, *HaShem*, our God and God of our forefathers, above and beyond all the song and praise expressed by David son of Yishai, Your servant and anointed one.

GLORIFY   GOD

יִשְׁתַּבַּח שִׁמְךָ לָעַד מַלְכֵּנוּ, הָאֵל הַמֶּלֶךְ הַגָּדוֹל וְהַקָּדוֹשׁ בַּשָּׁמַיִם וּבָאָרֶץ, כִּי לְךָ נָאֶה, יְהֹוָה אֱלֹהֵינוּ וֵאלֹהֵי אֲבוֹתֵינוּ, שִׁיר וּשְׁבָחָה, הַלֵּל וְזִמְרָה, עֹז וּמֶמְשָׁלָה, נֶצַח גְּדֻלָּה וּגְבוּרָה, תְּהִלָּה וְתִפְאֶרֶת, קְדֻשָּׁה וּמַלְכוּת, בְּרָכוֹת וְהוֹדָאוֹת מֵעַתָּה וְעַד עוֹלָם. בָּרוּךְ אַתָּה יְהֹוָה, אֵל מֶלֶךְ גָּדוֹל בַּתִּשְׁבָּחוֹת, אֵל הַהוֹדָאוֹת, אֲדוֹן הַנִּפְלָאוֹת, הַבּוֹחֵר בְּשִׁירֵי זִמְרָה, מֶלֶךְ אֵל חַי הָעוֹלָמִים.

Yishtabach shimkha la'ad malkeinu, ha'Eil hamelekh hagadol v'hakadosh bashamayim uva'aretz, ki l'kha na'e, Adonai Eloheinu vElohei avoteinu, shir ushvacha, haleil v'zimra, oz umemshala, netzach g'dula ugvura, t'hila v'tif'eret, k'dusha umalkhut, b'rakhot v'hoda'ot mei'ata v'ad olam. Barukh ata Adonai, Eil melekh gadol batishbachot, Eil hahoda'ot, adon hanifla'ot, habocheir b'shirei zimra, melekh Eil chai ha'olamim.

May Your name be praised forever, our Ruler, great and holy God, in heaven and on earth. Because You, *HaShem*, our God and God of our forefathers, are due song and praise; thanksgiving and paeans; power and dominion; triumph, greatness, and strength; prayer and glory; holiness and sovereignty; blessing and gratitude from now to eternity. Blessed are You, *HaShem*, God, Ruler, exalted in praise, God of thanksgiving, Master of wonders, who chooses songs of praise—Ruler, God, Lifegiver of the Universe.

THE · FOURTH · CUP

Pour yourself that fourth cup of wine, say the following blessing, and drink. Some people recline to the left as they do so, but you know that by now:

בָּרוּךְ אַתָּה יְהֹוָה אֱלֹהֵינוּ מֶלֶךְ הָעוֹלָם, בּוֹרֵא פְּרִי הַגָּפֶן.

Barukh ata Adonai Eloheinu melekh ha'olam, borei p'ri hagafen.

Blessed are You, *HaShem*, our God, Ruler of the Universe, who creates the fruit of the vine.

THANK   PRAISE   LAUD

בָּרוּךְ אַתָּה יְהֹוָה אֱלֹהֵינוּ מֶלֶךְ הָעוֹלָם, עַל הַגֶּפֶן וְעַל פְּרִי הַגֶּפֶן, עַל תְּנוּבַת הַשָּׂדֶה וְעַל אֶרֶץ חֶמְדָּה טוֹבָה וּרְחָבָה שֶׁרָצִיתָ וְהִנְחַלְתָּ לַאֲבוֹתֵינוּ, לֶאֱכֹל מִפִּרְיָהּ וְלִשְׂבֹּעַ מִטּוּבָהּ. רַחֵם נָא יְהֹוָה אֱלֹהֵינוּ עַל יִשְׂרָאֵל עַמֶּךָ, וְעַל יְרוּשָׁלַיִם עִירֶךָ, וְעַל צִיּוֹן מִשְׁכַּן כְּבוֹדֶךָ, וְעַל מִזְבְּחֶךָ וְעַל הֵיכָלֶךָ. וּבְנֵה יְרוּשָׁלַיִם עִיר הַקֹּדֶשׁ בִּמְהֵרָה בְיָמֵינוּ, וְהַעֲלֵנוּ לְתוֹכָהּ וְשַׂמְּחֵנוּ בְּבִנְיָנָהּ, וְנֹאכַל מִפִּרְיָהּ, וְנִשְׂבַּע מִטּוּבָהּ, וּנְבָרֶכְךָ עָלֶיהָ בִּקְדֻשָּׁה וּבְטָהֳרָה (בשבת: וּרְצֵה וְהַחֲלִיצֵנוּ בְּיוֹם הַשַּׁבָּת הַזֶּה) וְשַׂמְּחֵנוּ בְּיוֹם חַג הַמַּצּוֹת הַזֶּה, כִּי אַתָּה יְהֹוָה טוֹב וּמֵטִיב לַכֹּל וְנוֹדֶה לְּךָ עַל הָאָרֶץ וְעַל פְּרִי הַגֶּפֶן. בָּרוּךְ אַתָּה יְהֹוָה, עַל הָאָרֶץ וְעַל פְּרִי הַגֶּפֶן.

Barukh ata Adonai Eloheinu melekh ha'olam, al hagefen v'al p'ri hagefen, al t'nuvat hasade v'al eretz chemda tova urchava sheratzita v'hinchalta la'avoteinu, le'ekhol mipiryah v'lisbo'a mituvah. Rachem na Adonai Eloheinu al Yisra'eil amekha, v'al Y'rushalayim irekha, v'al Tziyon mishkan k'vodekha, v'al mizb'chekha v'al heikhalekha. Uvnei Y'rushalayim ir hakodesh bimheira v'yameinu, v'ha'aleinu l'tokhah v'sam'cheinu b'vinyanah, v'nokhal mipiryah, v'nisba mituvah, unvarekh'kha aleha bikdusha uvtohora (On Shabbat add: urtzei v'hachalitzeinu b'yom haShabbat haze) v'sam'cheinu b'yom chag hamatzahs haze, ki ata Adonai tov umeitiv lakol v'node l'kha al ha'aretz v'al p'ri hagefen. Barukh ata Adonai, al ha'aretz v'al p'ri hagefen.

Blessed are You, *HaShem*, our God, Ruler of the Universe, for the vine and fruit of the vine, for the produce of the field, for the desirable, good, and spacious land that you were pleased to grant to our forefathers to eat of its fruit and be sated by its bounty. Please have mercy, *HaShem*, our God, on Israel Your people, on Jerusalem Your city, on Zion the abode of Your glory, on Your altar, and on Your Temple. Rebuild Your holy city of Jerusalem speedily, in our days, and bring us into it, gladden us in its rebuilding; let us eat from its fruit, be sated by its bounty, and bless you for it in holiness and purity. [*On Shabbat add:* Favor and strengthen us on this Shabbat day and] gladden us on this Festival of Matzahs, for You, *HaShem*, are good and do good to all, and we thank You for the land and for the fruit of the vine. Blessed are You, *HaShem*, for the land and for the fruit of the vine.

Nirtzah

This is it. We've reached the end. Before we sing some songs or succumb to sleep, we need to declare the Seder officially over:

חֲסַל סִדּוּר פֶּסַח כְּהִלְכָתוֹ, כְּכָל מִשְׁפָּטוֹ וְחֻקָּתוֹ. כַּאֲשֶׁר זָכִינוּ לְסַדֵּר אוֹתוֹ, כֵּן נִזְכֶּה לַעֲשׂוֹתוֹ. זָךְ שׁוֹכֵן מְעוֹנָה, קוֹמֵם קְהַל עֲדַת מִי מָנָה. בְּקָרוֹב נַהֵל נִטְעֵי כַנָּה, פְּדוּיִם לְצִיּוֹן בְּרִנָּה.

Chasal sidur Pesach k'hilkhato, k'khol mishpato v'chukato. Ka'asher zakhinu l'sadeir oto, kein nizke la'asoto. Zakh shokhein m'ona, komeim k'hal adat mi mana. B'karov naheil nit'ei khana, p'duyim l'Tziyon b'rina.

The Pesach Seder has been completed properly, according to all its laws and rules. Just as we were privileged to celebrate it, so may we merit to perform it. May the Pure One who dwells in heaven raise up the innumerable congregation, and very soon lead the offshoots of the planted stock, redeemed, to Zion in joy.

לְשָׁנָה הַבָּאָה בִּירוּשָׁלָיִם.

L'shana haba'a biYrushalayim.

Next year in Jerusalem!

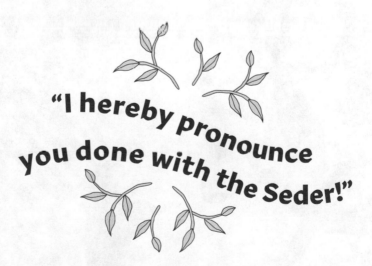

"I hereby pronounce you done with the Seder!"

The After-Party

Hatikvah

As rebuilt Jerusalem is, well, built, many Jews conclude the
Seder by singing "Hatikvah," Israel's national anthem:

1   כֹּל עוֹד בַּלֵּבָב פְּנִימָה

2   נֶפֶשׁ יְהוּדִי הוֹמִיָּה.

3   וּלְפַאֲתֵי מִזְרָח, קָדִימָה,

4   עַיִן לְצִיּוֹן צוֹפִיָּה.

5   עוֹד לֹא אָבְדָה תִּקְוָתֵנוּ,

6   הַתִּקְוָה בַּת שְׁנוֹת אַלְפַּיִם,

7   לִהְיוֹת עַם חָפְשִׁי בְּאַרְצֵנוּ,

8   אֶרֶץ צִיּוֹן וִירוּשָׁלַיִם.

Go to tabletmag.com/haggadah for the tune.

1 As long as deep within the heart	1 Kol od baleivav p'nima
2 A Jewish soul stirs,	2 Nefesh Y'hudi homiya.
3 And forward, to the ends of the East	3 Ulfa'atei mizrach kadima,
4 An eye looks out, expectantly, toward Zion—	4 Ayin l'Tziyon tzofiya.
5 Our hope is not yet lost,	5 Od lo av'da tikvateinu,
6 The hope of two thousand years,	6 Hatikvah bat sh'not alpayim
7 To be a free people in our land	7 Lihyot am chofshi b'artzeinu
8 The land of Zion and Jerusalem.	8 Eretz Tziyon viYrushalayim

Go down, Moses? Or not? Anthony Mordechai Tzvi Russell explores our history, and his own (page 140).

Just as we did with the four questions that launched tonight's Seder, we again seek here to engage in a cycle of asking and answering questions—but now, of course, there's the challenge of also keeping everyone awake. So we sing!

The following two songs are both alphabet mnemonics, moving through the Hebrew aleph-bet one letter at a time with each new phrase.

Ki Lo Na'eh

This hymn was originally intended for the first night of Passover, with "Adir Hu" (page 118) as its second-night partner. This seems to have been too complicated to maintain. After centuries of confusion, both are now regularly sung on both nights.

1 כִּי לוֹ נָאֶה, כִּי לוֹ יָאֶה.

2 אַדִּיר בִּמְלוּכָה, בָּחוּר כַּהֲלָכָה, גְּדוּדָיו יֹאמְרוּ לוֹ:
לְךָ וּלְךָ, לְךָ כִּי לְךָ, לְךָ אַף לְךָ, לְךָ יְהֹוָה הַמַּמְלָכָה.
כִּי לוֹ נָאֶה, כִּי לוֹ יָאֶה.

3 דָּגוּל בִּמְלוּכָה, הָדוּר כַּהֲלָכָה, וָתִיקָיו יֹאמְרוּ לוֹ:
לְךָ וּלְךָ, לְךָ כִּי לְךָ, לְךָ אַף לְךָ, לְךָ יְהֹוָה הַמַּמְלָכָה.
כִּי לוֹ נָאֶה, כִּי לוֹ יָאֶה.

4 זַכַּאי בִּמְלוּכָה, חָסִין כַּהֲלָכָה, טַפְסְרָיו יֹאמְרוּ לוֹ:
לְךָ וּלְךָ, לְךָ כִּי לְךָ, לְךָ אַף לְךָ, לְךָ יְהֹוָה הַמַּמְלָכָה.
כִּי לוֹ נָאֶה, כִּי לוֹ יָאֶה.

5 יָחִיד בִּמְלוּכָה, כַּבִּיר כַּהֲלָכָה, לִמּוּדָיו יֹאמְרוּ לוֹ:
לְךָ וּלְךָ, לְךָ כִּי לְךָ, לְךָ אַף לְךָ, לְךָ יְהֹוָה הַמַּמְלָכָה.
כִּי לוֹ נָאֶה, כִּי לוֹ יָאֶה.

6 מוֹשֵׁל בִּמְלוּכָה, נוֹרָא כַּהֲלָכָה, סְבִיבָיו יֹאמְרוּ לוֹ:
לְךָ וּלְךָ, לְךָ כִּי לְךָ, לְךָ אַף לְךָ, לְךָ יְהֹוָה הַמַּמְלָכָה.
כִּי לוֹ נָאֶה, כִּי לוֹ יָאֶה.

7 עָנָו בִּמְלוּכָה, פּוֹדֶה כַּהֲלָכָה, צַדִּיקָיו יֹאמְרוּ לוֹ:
לְךָ וּלְךָ, לְךָ כִּי לְךָ, לְךָ אַף לְךָ, לְךָ יְהֹוָה הַמַּמְלָכָה.

8 קָדוֹשׁ בִּמְלוּכָה, רַחוּם כַּהֲלָכָה, שִׁנְאַנָּיו יֹאמְרוּ לוֹ:
לְךָ וּלְךָ, לְךָ כִּי לְךָ, לְךָ אַף לְךָ, לְךָ יְהֹוָה הַמַּמְלָכָה.
כִּי לוֹ נָאֶה, כִּי לוֹ יָאֶה.

9 תַּקִּיף בִּמְלוּכָה, תּוֹמֵךְ כַּהֲלָכָה, תְּמִימָיו יֹאמְרוּ לוֹ:
לְךָ וּלְךָ, לְךָ כִּי לְךָ, לְךָ אַף לְךָ, לְךָ יְהֹוָה הַמַּמְלָכָה.
כִּי לוֹ נָאֶה, כִּי לוֹ יָאֶה.

Go to
tabletmag.com/haggadah
for the tune.

1 Because it is due Him,
because it befits Him.

1 Ki lo na'e, ki lo ya'e.

---

2 Mighty in sovereignty, rightly select. His minions say to Him: "Yours and truly Yours, Yours because it is Yours, Yours and only Yours—Yours, *HaShem*, is sovereignty!"
Because it is due Him,
because it befits Him.

2 Adir bimlukha, bachur kahalakha,
g'dudav yom'ru lo:
L'kha ulkha, l'kha ki l'kha, l'kha af l'kha,
l'kha Adonai hamamlakha.
Ki lo na'e, ki lo ya'e.

---

3 Exalted in sovereignty, rightly glorious. His faithful ones say to Him: "Yours and truly Yours, Yours because it is Yours, Yours and only Yours—Yours, *HaShem*, is sovereignty!"
Because it is due Him,
because it befits Him.

3 Dagul bimlukha, hadur kahalakha,
vatikav yom'ru lo:
L'kha ulkha, l'kha ki l'kha, l'kha af l'kha,
l'kha Adonai hamamlakha.
Ki lo na'e, ki lo ya'e.

---

4 Blameless in sovereignty, rightly powerful. His generals say to Him: "Yours and truly Yours, Yours because it is Yours, Yours and only Yours—Yours, *HaShem*, is sovereignty!"
Because it is due Him,
because it befits Him.

4 Zakai bimlukha, chasin kahalakha,
tafs'rav yom'ru lo:
L'kha ulkha, l'kha ki l'kha, l'kha af l'kha,
l'kha Adonai hamamlakha.
Ki lo na'e, ki lo ya'e.

---

5 Singular in sovereignty, rightly strong. His learned ones say to Him: "Yours and truly Yours, Yours because it is Yours, Yours and only Yours—Yours, *HaShem*, is sovereignty!"
Because it is due Him,
because it befits Him.

5 Yachid bimlukha, kabir kahalakha,
limudav yom'ru lo:
L'kha ulkha, l'kha ki l'kha, l'kha af l'kha,
l'kha Adonai hamamlakha.
Ki lo na'e, ki lo ya'e.

---

6 Commanding in sovereignty, rightly awesome. Those who surround Him say to Him: "Yours and truly Yours, Yours because it is Yours, Yours and only Yours—Yours, *HaShem*, is sovereignty!"
Because it is due Him,
because it befits Him.

6 Mosheil bimlukha, nora kahalakha,
s'vivav yom'ru lo:
L'kha ulkha, l'kha ki l'kha, l'kha af l'kha,
l'kha Adonai hamamlakha.
Ki lo na'e, ki lo ya'e.

---

7 Humble in sovereignty, rightly saving. His righteous ones say to Him: "Yours and truly Yours, Yours because it is Yours, Yours and only Yours—Yours, *HaShem*, is sovereignty!"
Because it is due Him,
because it befits Him.

7 Anav bimlukha, pode kahalakha,
tzadikav yom'ru lo:
L'kha ulkha, l'kha ki l'kha, l'kha af l'kha,
l'kha Adonai hamamlakha.
Ki lo na'e, ki lo ya'e.

---

8 Holy in sovereignty, rightly merciful. His multitudes say to Him: "Yours and truly Yours, Yours because it is Yours, Yours and only Yours—Yours, *HaShem*, is sovereignty!"
Because it is due Him,
because it befits Him.

8 Kadosh bimlukha, rachum kahalakha,
shin-anav yom'ru lo:
L'kha ulkha, l'kha ki l'kha, l'kha af l'kha,
l'kha Adonai hamamlakha.
Ki lo na'e, ki lo ya'e.

---

9 Strong in sovereignty, rightly supportive. His perfect ones say to Him: "Yours and truly Yours, Yours because it is Yours, Yours and only Yours—Yours, *HaShem*, is sovereignty!"
Because it is due Him,
because it befits Him.

9 Takif bimlukha, tomeikh kahalakha,
t'mimav yom'ru lo:
L'kha ulkha, l'kha ki l'kha, l'kha af l'kha,
l'kha Adonai hamamlakha.
Ki lo na'e, ki lo ya'e.

Adir Hu

Like its partner song, "Ki Lo Na'eh" (page 116), this hymn also dates back to the fifteenth century. Sing 'em on both nights, out of respect for the happy accidents of history.

1. אַדִּיר הוּא, יִבְנֶה בֵיתוֹ בְּקָרוֹב.
בִּמְהֵרָה, בִּמְהֵרָה, בְּיָמֵינוּ בְּקָרוֹב.
אֵל בְּנֵה, אֵל בְּנֵה, בְּנֵה בֵיתְךָ בְּקָרוֹב.

2. בָּחוּר הוּא, גָּדוֹל הוּא, דָּגוּל הוּא, יִבְנֶה בֵיתוֹ בְּקָרוֹב.
בִּמְהֵרָה, בִּמְהֵרָה, בְּיָמֵינוּ בְּקָרוֹב.
אֵל בְּנֵה, אֵלבְּנֵה, בְּנֵה בֵיתְךָ בְּקָרוֹב.

3. הָדוּר הוּא, וָתִיק הוּא, זַכַּאי הוּא, יִבְנֶה בֵיתוֹ בְּקָרוֹב.
בִּמְהֵרָה, בִּמְהֵרָה, בְּיָמֵינוּ בְּקָרוֹב.
אֵל בְּנֵה, אֵלבְּנֵה, בְּנֵה בֵיתְךָ בְּקָרוֹב.

4. חָסִיד הוּא, טָהוֹר הוּא, יָחִיד הוּא, יִבְנֶה בֵיתוֹ בְּקָרוֹב.
בִּמְהֵרָה, בִּמְהֵרָה, בְּיָמֵינוּ בְּקָרוֹב.
אֵל בְּנֵה, אֵלבְּנֵה, בְּנֵה בֵיתְךָ בְּקָרוֹב.

5. כַּבִּיר הוּא, לָמוּד הוּא, מֶלֶךְ הוּא, יִבְנֶה בֵיתוֹ בְּקָרוֹב.
בִּמְהֵרָה, בִּמְהֵרָה, בְּיָמֵינוּ בְּקָרוֹב.
אֵל בְּנֵה, אֵלבְּנֵה, בְּנֵה בֵיתְךָ בְּקָרוֹב.

6. נוֹרָא הוּא, סַגִּיב הוּא, עִזּוּז הוּא, יִבְנֶה בֵיתוֹ בְּקָרוֹב.
בִּמְהֵרָה, בִּמְהֵרָה, בְּיָמֵינוּ בְּקָרוֹב.
אֵל בְּנֵה, אֵלבְּנֵה, בְּנֵה בֵיתְךָ בְּקָרוֹב.

7. פּוֹדֶה הוּא, צַדִּיק הוּא, קָדוֹשׁ הוּא, יִבְנֶה בֵיתוֹ בְּקָרוֹב.
בִּמְהֵרָה, בִּמְהֵרָה, בְּיָמֵינוּ בְּקָרוֹב.
אֵל בְּנֵה, אֵלבְּנֵה, בְּנֵה בֵיתְךָ בְּקָרוֹב.

8. רַחוּם הוּא, שַׁדַּי הוּא, תַּקִּיף הוּא, יִבְנֶה בֵיתוֹ בְּקָרוֹב.
בִּמְהֵרָה, בִּמְהֵרָה, בְּיָמֵינוּ בְּקָרוֹב.
אֵל בְּנֵה, אֵלבְּנֵה, בְּנֵה בֵיתְךָ בְּקָרוֹב.

1 He is mighty. May He rebuild His house soon! Speedily, speedily, in our days, soon! God, rebuild! God, rebuild! Rebuild Your house soon!

2 He is distinguished. He is great. He is lofty. May He rebuild His house soon! Speedily, speedily, in our days, soon! God, rebuild! God, rebuild! Rebuild Your house soon!

3 He is glorious. He is faithful. He is blameless. May He rebuild His house soon! Speedily, speedily, in our days, soon! God, rebuild! God, rebuild! Rebuild Your house soon!

4 He is righteous. He is pure. He is singular. May He rebuild His house soon! Speedily, speedily, in our days, soon! God, rebuild! God, rebuild! Rebuild Your house soon!

5 He is powerful. He is omniscient. He is king. May He rebuild His house soon! Speedily, speedily, in our days, soon! God, rebuild! God, rebuild! Rebuild Your house soon!

6 He is awesome. He is sublime. He is omnipotent. May He rebuild His house soon! Speedily, speedily, in our days, soon! God, rebuild! God, rebuild! Rebuild Your house soon!

7 He is salvific. He is just. He is holy. May He rebuild His house soon! Speedily, speedily, in our days, soon! God, rebuild! God, rebuild! Rebuild Your house soon!

8 He is merciful. He is Almighty. He is strong. May He rebuild His house soon! Speedily, speedily, in our days, soon! God, rebuild! God, rebuild! Rebuild Your house soon!

1 Adir hu, yivne veito b'karov.
Bimheira, bimheira, b'yameinu b'karov.
Eil b'nei, Eil b'nei, b'nei veit'kha b'karov.

2 Bachur hu, gadol hu, dagul hu, yivne veito b'karov.
Bimheira, bimheira, b'yameinu b'karov.
Eil b'nei, Eil b'nei, b'nei veit'kha b'karov.

3 Hadur hu, vatik hu, zakai hu, yivne veito b'karov.
Bimheira, bimheira, b'yameinu b'karov.
Eil b'nei, Eil b'nei, b'nei veit'kha b'karov.

4 Chasid hu, tahor hu, yachid hu, yivne veito b'karov.
Bimheira, bimheira, b'yameinu b'karov.
Eil b'nei, Eil b'nei, b'nei veit'kha b'karov.

5 Kabir hu, lamud hu, melekh hu, yivne veito b'karov.
Bimheira, bimheira, b'yameinu b'karov.
Eil b'nei, Eil b'nei, b'nei veit'kha b'karov.

6 Nora hu, sagiv hu, izuz hu, yivne veito b'karov.
Bimheira, bimheira, b'yameinu b'karov.
Eil b'nei, Eil b'nei, b'nei veit'kha b'karov.

7 Pode hu, tzadik hu, kadosh hu, yivne veito b'karov.
Bimheira, bimheira, b'yameinu b'karov.
Eil b'nei, Eil b'nei, b'nei veit'kha b'karov.

8 Rachum hu, Shadai hu, takif hu, yivne veito b'karov.
Bimheira, bimheira, b'yameinu b'karov.
Eil b'nei, Eil b'nei, b'nei veit'kha b'karov.

Echad Mi Yode'a

First appearing in German Haggadot sometime in the fifteenth century, this *piyut*, or liturgical song, is meant to be a fun and humorous way to enumerate the central tenets of the Jewish faith, counting from the one almighty God to the thirteen attributes of Divine mercy.

Give everyone around the table a different number to recite.

1 אֶחָד מִי יוֹדֵעַ, אֶחָד אֲנִי יוֹדֵעַ.
אֶחָד אֱלֹהֵינוּ שֶׁבַּשָּׁמַיִם וּבָאָרֶץ:

2 שְׁנַיִם מִי יוֹדֵעַ, שְׁנַיִם אֲנִי יוֹדֵעַ.
שְׁנֵי לֻחוֹת הַבְּרִית. אֶחָד אֱלֹהֵינוּ שֶׁבַּשָּׁמַיִם וּבָאָרֶץ:

3 שְׁלֹשָׁה מִי יוֹדֵעַ, שְׁלֹשָׁה אֲנִי יוֹדֵעַ.
שְׁלֹשָׁה אָבוֹת, שְׁנֵי לֻחוֹת הַבְּרִית,
אֶחָד אֱלֹהֵינוּ שֶׁבַּשָּׁמַיִם וּבָאָרֶץ:

4 אַרְבַּע מִי יוֹדֵעַ, אַרְבַּע אֲנִי יוֹדֵעַ.
אַרְבַּע אִמָּהוֹת, שְׁלֹשָׁה אָבוֹת, שְׁנֵי לֻחוֹת הַבְּרִית,
אֶחָד אֱלֹהֵינוּ שֶׁבַּשָּׁמַיִם וּבָאָרֶץ:

5 חֲמִשָּׁה מִי יוֹדֵעַ, חֲמִשָּׁה אֲנִי יוֹדֵעַ.
חֲמִשָּׁה חוּמְשֵׁי תוֹרָה, אַרְבַּע אִמָּהוֹת, שְׁלֹשָׁה אָבוֹת,
שְׁנֵי לֻחוֹת הַבְּרִית, אֶחָד אֱלֹהֵינוּ שֶׁבַּשָּׁמַיִם וּבָאָרֶץ:

6 שִׁשָּׁה מִי יוֹדֵעַ, שִׁשָּׁה אֲנִי יוֹדֵעַ.
שִׁשָּׁה סִדְרֵי מִשְׁנָה, חֲמִשָּׁה חוּמְשֵׁי תוֹרָה, אַרְבַּע אִמָּהוֹת, שְׁלֹשָׁה אָבוֹת,
שְׁנֵי לֻחוֹת הַבְּרִית, אֶחָד אֱלֹהֵינוּ שֶׁבַּשָּׁמַיִם וּבָאָרֶץ:

7 שִׁבְעָה מִי יוֹדֵעַ, שִׁבְעָה אֲנִי יוֹדֵעַ.
שִׁבְעָה יְמֵי שַׁבַּתָּא, שִׁשָּׁה סִדְרֵי מִשְׁנָה, חֲמִשָּׁה חוּמְשֵׁי תוֹרָה,
אַרְבַּע אִמָּהוֹת, שְׁלֹשָׁה אָבוֹת, שְׁנֵי לֻחוֹת הַבְּרִית,
אֶחָד אֱלֹהֵינוּ שֶׁבַּשָּׁמַיִם וּבָאָרֶץ:

8 שְׁמוֹנָה מִי יוֹדֵעַ, שְׁמוֹנָה אֲנִי יוֹדֵעַ.
שְׁמוֹנָה יְמֵי מִילָה, שִׁבְעָה יְמֵי שַׁבַּתָּא, שִׁשָּׁה סִדְרֵי מִשְׁנָה,
חֲמִשָּׁה חוּמְשֵׁי תוֹרָה, אַרְבַּע אִמָּהוֹת, שְׁלֹשָׁה אָבוֹת, שְׁנֵי לֻחוֹת הַבְּרִית,
אֶחָד אֱלֹהֵינוּ שֶׁבַּשָּׁמַיִם וּבָאָרֶץ:

Go to tabletmag.com/haggadah for the tune.

1 Who knows one? I know one. One is our God in heaven and on Earth.

2 **Who knows two?** I know two. Two are the tablets of the covenant. One is our God in heaven and on Earth.

3 Who knows three? I know three. Three are the patriarchs. Two are the tablets of the covenant. One is our God in heaven and on Earth.

4 **Who knows four?** I know four. Four are the matriarchs. Three are the patriarchs. Two are the tablets of the covenant. One is our God in heaven and on Earth.

5 **Who knows five?** I know five. Five are the books of the Torah. Four are the matriarchs. Three are the patriarchs. Two are the tablets of the covenant. One is our God in heaven and on Earth.

6 **Who knows six?** I know six. Six are the orders of the Mishnah. Five are the books of the Torah. Four are the matriarchs. Three are the patriarchs. Two are the tablets of the covenant. One is our God in heaven and on Earth.

7 **Who knows seven?** I know seven. Seven are the days of the week. Six are the orders of the Mishnah. Five are the books of the Torah. Four are the matriarchs. Three are the patriarchs. Two are the tablets of the covenant. One is our God in heaven and on Earth.

8 **Who knows eight?** I know eight. Eight are the days for circumcision. Seven are the days of the week. Six are the orders of the Mishnah. Five are the books of the Torah. Four are the matriarchs. Three are the patriarchs. Two are the tablets of the covenant. One is our God in heaven and on Earth.

1 Echad mi yode'a, echad ani yode'a. Echad Eloheinu shebashamayim uva'aretz.

2 Sh'nayim mi yode'a, sh'nayim ani yode'a. Sh'nei luchot hab'rit, echad Eloheinu shebashamayim uva'aretz.

3 Sh'losha mi yode'a, sh'losha ani yode'a. Sh'losha avot, sh'nei luchot hab'rit, echad Eloheinu shebashamayim uva'aretz.

4 Arba mi yode'a, arba ani yode'a. Arba Imahot, sh'losha avot, sh'nei luchot hab'rit, echad Eloheinu shebashamayim uva'aretz.

5 Chamisha mi yode'a, chamisha ani yode'a. Chamisha chumshei Tora, arba imahot, sh'losha avot, sh'nei luchot hab'rit, echad Eloheinu shebashamayim uva'aretz.

6 Shisha mi yode'a, shisha ani yode'a. Shisha sidrei Mishna, chamisha chumshei Tora, arba imahot, sh'losha avot, sh'nei luchot hab'rit, echad Eloheinu shebashamayim uva'aretz.

7 Shiv'a mi yode'a, shiv'a ani yode'a. Shiv'a y'mei shab'ta, shisha sidrei Mishna, chamisha chumshei Tora, arba imahot, sh'losha avot, sh'nei luchot hab'rit, echad Eloheinu shebashamayim uva'aretz.

8 Sh'mona mi yode'a, sh'mona ani yode'a. Sh'mona y'mei mila, shiv'a y'mei shab'ta, shisha sidrei Mishna, chamisha chumshei Tora, arba imahot, sh'losha avot, sh'nei luchot hab'rit, echad Eloheinu shebashamayim uva'aretz.

9 תִּשְׁעָה מִי יוֹדֵעַ, תִּשְׁעָה אֲנִי יוֹדֵעַ.
תִּשְׁעָה יַרְחֵי לֵידָה, שְׁמוֹנָה יְמֵי מִילָה, שִׁבְעָה יְמֵי שַׁבַּתָּא, שִׁשָּׁה סִדְרֵי
מִשְׁנָה, חֲמִשָּׁה חוּמְשֵׁי תוֹרָה, אַרְבַּע אִמָּהוֹת, שְׁלֹשָׁה אָבוֹת,
שְׁנֵי לֻחוֹת הַבְּרִית, אֶחָד אֱלֹהֵינוּ שֶׁבַּשָּׁמַיִם וּבָאָרֶץ:

10 עֲשָׂרָה מִי יוֹדֵעַ, עֲשָׂרָה אֲנִי יוֹדֵעַ.
עֲשָׂרָה דִבְּרַיָּא, תִּשְׁעָה יַרְחֵי לֵידָה, שְׁמוֹנָה יְמֵי מִילָה, שִׁבְעָה יְמֵי שַׁבַּתָּא,
שִׁשָּׁה סִדְרֵי מִשְׁנָה, חֲמִשָּׁה חוּמְשֵׁי תוֹרָה, אַרְבַּע אִמָּהוֹת, שְׁלֹשָׁה אָבוֹת,
שְׁנֵי לֻחוֹת הַבְּרִית, אֶחָד אֱלֹהֵינוּ שֶׁבַּשָּׁמַיִם וּבָאָרֶץ:

11 אַחַד עָשָׂר מִי יוֹדֵעַ, אַחַד עָשָׂר אֲנִי יוֹדֵעַ.
אַחַד עָשָׂר כּוֹכְבַיָּא, עֲשָׂרָה דִבְּרַיָּא, תִּשְׁעָה יַרְחֵי לֵידָה, שְׁמוֹנָה יְמֵי מִילָה,
שִׁבְעָה יְמֵי שַׁבַּתָּא, שִׁשָּׁה סִדְרֵי מִשְׁנָה, חֲמִשָּׁה חוּמְשֵׁי תוֹרָה,
אַרְבַּע אִמָּהוֹת, שְׁלֹשָׁה אָבוֹת, שְׁנֵי לֻחוֹת הַבְּרִית,
אֶחָד אֱלֹהֵינוּ שֶׁבַּשָּׁמַיִם וּבָאָרֶץ:

12 שְׁנֵים עָשָׂר מִי יוֹדֵעַ, שְׁנֵים עָשָׂר אֲנִי יוֹדֵעַ.
שְׁנֵים עָשָׂר שִׁבְטַיָּא, אַחַד עָשָׂר כּוֹכְבַיָּא, עֲשָׂרָה דִבְּרַיָּא, תִּשְׁעָה יַרְחֵי
לֵידָה, שְׁמוֹנָה יְמֵי מִילָה, שִׁבְעָה יְמֵי שַׁבַּתָּא, שִׁשָּׁה סִדְרֵי מִשְׁנָה,
חֲמִשָּׁה חוּמְשֵׁי תוֹרָה, אַרְבַּע אִמָּהוֹת, שְׁלֹשָׁה אָבוֹת, שְׁנֵי לֻחוֹת הַבְּרִית,
אֶחָד אֱלֹהֵינוּ שֶׁבַּשָּׁמַיִם וּבָאָרֶץ:

13 שְׁלֹשָׁה עָשָׂר מִי יוֹדֵעַ, שְׁלֹשָׁה עָשָׂר אֲנִי יוֹדֵעַ.
שְׁלֹשָׁה עָשָׂר מִדַּיָּא. שְׁנֵים עָשָׂר שִׁבְטַיָּא, אַחַד עָשָׂר כּוֹכְבַיָּא,
עֲשָׂרָה דִבְּרַיָּא, תִּשְׁעָה יַרְחֵי לֵידָה, שְׁמוֹנָה יְמֵי מִילָה,
שִׁבְעָה יְמֵי שַׁבַּתָּא, שִׁשָּׁה סִדְרֵי מִשְׁנָה, חֲמִשָּׁה חוּמְשֵׁי תוֹרָה,
אַרְבַּע אִמָּהוֹת, שְׁלֹשָׁה אָבוֹת, שְׁנֵי לֻחוֹת הַבְּרִית,
אֶחָד אֱלֹהֵינוּ שֶׁבַּשָּׁמַיִם וּבָאָרֶץ:

9 **Who knows nine?** I know nine. Nine are the months of childbirth. Eight are the days for circumcision. Seven are the days of the week. Six are the orders of the Mishnah. Five are the books of the Torah. Four are the matriarchs. Three are the patriarchs. Two are the tablets of the covenant. One is our God in heaven and on Earth.

10 **Who knows ten?** I know ten. Ten are the Commandments from Sinai. Nine are the months of childbirth. Eight are the days for circumcision. Seven are the days of the week. Six are the orders of the Mishnah. Five are the books of the Torah. Four are the matriarchs. Three are the patriarchs. Two are the tablets of the covenant. One is our God in heaven and on Earth.

11 **Who knows eleven?** I know eleven. Eleven are the stars [in Joseph's dream]. Ten are the Commandments from Sinai. Nine are the months of childbirth. Eight are the days for circumcision. Seven are the days of the week. Six are the orders of the Mishnah. Five are the books of the Torah. Four are the matriarchs. Three are the patriarchs. Two are the tablets of the covenant. One is our God in heaven and on Earth.

12 **Who knows twelve?** I know twelve. Twelve are the tribes. Eleven are the stars [in Joseph's dream]. Ten are the Commandments from Sinai. Nine are the months of childbirth. Eight are the days for circumcision. Seven are the days of the week. Six are the orders of the Mishnah. Five are the books of the Torah. Four are the matriarchs. Three are the patriarchs. Two are the tablets of the covenant. One is our God in heaven and on Earth.

13 **Who knows thirteen?** I know thirteen. Thirteen are the Attributes of God. Twelve are the tribes. Eleven are the stars [in Joseph's dream]. Ten are the Commandments from Sinai. Nine are the months of childbirth. Eight are the days for circumcision. Seven are the days of the week. Six are the orders of the Mishnah. Five are the books of the Torah. Four are the matriarchs. Three are the patriarchs. Two are the tablets of the covenant. One is our God in heaven and on Earth.

9   Tish'a mi yode'a, tish'a ani yode'a. Tish'a yarchei leida, sh'mona y'mei mila, shiv'a y'mei shab'ta, shisha sidrei Mishna, chamisha chumshei Tora, arba imahot, sh'losha avot, sh'nei luchot hab'rit, echad Eloheinu shebashamayim uva'aretz.

10   Asara mi yode'a, asara ani yode'a. Asara dib'raya, tish'a yarchei leida, sh'mona y'mei mila, shiv'a y'mei shab'ta, shisha sidrei Mishna, chamisha chumshei Tora, arba imahot, sh'losha avot, sh'nei luchot hab'rit, echad Eloheinu shebashamayim uva'aretz.

11   Achad-asar mi yode'a, achad-asar ani yode'a. Achad-asar kokh'vaya, asara dib'raya, tish'a yarchei leida, sh'mona y'mei mila, shiv'a y'mei shab'ta, shisha sidrei Mishna, chamisha chumshei Tora, arba imahot, sh'losha avot, sh'nei luchot hab'rit, echad Eloheinu shebashamayim uva'aretz.

12   Sh'neim-asar mi yode'a, sh'neim-asar ani yode'a. Sh'neim-asar shivtaya, achad-asar kokh'vaya, asara dib'raya, tish'a yarchei leida, sh'mona y'mei mila, shiv'a y'mei shab'ta, shisha sidrei Mishna, chamisha chumshei Tora, arba imahot, sh'losha avot, sh'nei luchot hab'rit, echad Eloheinu shebashamayim uva'aretz.

13   Sh'losha-asar mi yode'a, sh'losha-asar ani yode'a. Sh'losha-asar midaya, sh'neim-asar shivtaya, achad-asar kokh'vaya, asara dib'raya, tish'a yarchei leida, sh'mona y'mei mila, shiv'a y'mei shab'ta, shisha sidrei Mishna, chamisha chumshei Tora, arba imahot, sh'losha avot, sh'nei luchot hab'rit, echad Eloheinu shebashamayim uva'aretz.

Chad Gadya

This song first appeared in the Prague Haggadah in 1590. It's a cyclical story about killing—the cat eats the kid goat, the dog bites the cat, the stick hits the dog, and so on—that ends only with the appearance of the Almighty, the one force in the universe that no other can subdue. Written in Aramaic, it was often understood by Jews in exile as an invitation to be patient: The empires of the world may fight each other to the death, but only God will prevail in the end.

1 חַד גַּדְיָא, חַד גַּדְיָא דְּזַבִּין אַבָּא בִּתְרֵי זוּזֵי.
חַד גַּדְיָא, חַד גַּדְיָא.

2 וְאָתָא שׁוּנְרָא וְאָכְלָה לְגַדְיָא, דְּזַבִּין אַבָּא בִּתְרֵי זוּזֵי.
חַד גַּדְיָא, חַד גַּדְיָא.

3 וְאָתָא כַלְבָּא וְנָשַׁךְ לְשׁוּנְרָא, דְּאָכְלָה לְגַדְיָא,
דְּזַבִּין אַבָּא בִּתְרֵי זוּזֵי. חַד גַּדְיָא, חַד גַּדְיָא.

4 וְאָתָא חוּטְרָא וְהִכָּה לְכַלְבָּא, דְּנָשַׁךְ לְשׁוּנְרָא,
דְּאָכְלָה לְגַדְיָא, דְּזַבִּין אַבָּא בִּתְרֵי זוּזֵי.
חַד גַּדְיָא, חַד גַּדְיָא.

5 וְאָתָא נוּרָא וְשָׂרַף לְחוּטְרָא, דְּהִכָּה לְכַלְבָּא,
דְּנָשַׁךְ לְשׁוּנְרָא, דְּאָכְלָה לְגַדְיָא, דְּזַבִּין אַבָּא בִּתְרֵי זוּזֵי.
חַד גַּדְיָא, חַד גַּדְיָא.

6 וְאָתָא מַיָּא וְכָבָה לְנוּרָא, דְּשָׂרַף לְחוּטְרָא, דְּהִכָּה לְכַלְבָּא,
דְּנָשַׁךְ לְשׁוּנְרָא, דְּאָכְלָה לְגַדְיָא, דְּזַבִּין אַבָּא בִּתְרֵי זוּזֵי.
חַד גַּדְיָא, חַד גַּדְיָא.

7 וְאָתָא תוֹרָא וְשָׁתָה לְמַיָּא, דְּכָבָה לְנוּרָא,
דְּשָׂרַף לְחוּטְרָא, דְּהִכָּה לְכַלְבָּא, דְּנָשַׁךְ לְשׁוּנְרָא,
דְּאָכְלָה לְגַדְיָא, דְּזַבִּין אַבָּא בִּתְרֵי זוּזֵי.
חַד גַּדְיָא, חַד גַּדְיָא.

A FUN SONG ABOUT MURDER

Go to tabletmag.com/haggadah for the tune.

1 One kid, one kid, that my father bought for two *zuz*, one kid, one kid.

2 Then came a cat and ate the kid, that my father bought for two *zuz*, one kid, one kid.

3 Then came a dog and bit the cat, that ate the kid, that my father bought for two *zuz*, one kid, one kid.

4 Then came a stick and hit the dog, that bit the cat, that ate the kid, that my father bought for two *zuz*, one kid, one kid.

5 Then came a fire and burnt the stick, that hit the dog, that bit the cat, that ate the kid, that my father bought for two *zuz*, one kid, one kid.

6 Then came water and put out the fire, that burnt the stick, that hit the dog, that bit the cat, that ate the kid, that my father bought for two *zuz*, one kid, one kid.

7 Then came a bull and drank up the water, that put out the fire, that burnt the stick, that hit the dog, that bit the cat, that ate the kid, that my father bought for two *zuz*, one kid, one kid.

1 Chad gadya, chad gadya, d'zabin aba bitrei zuzei. Chad gadya, chad gadya.

2 V'ata shun'ra v'akh'la l'gadya, d'zabin aba bitrei zuzei. Chad gadya, chad gadya.

3 V'ata kalba v'nashakh l'shun'ra, d'akh'la l'gadya, d'zabin aba bitrei zuzei. Chad gadya, chad gadya.

4 V'ata chutra v'hika l'khalba d'nashakh l'shun'ra, d'akh'la l'gadya, d'zabin aba bitrei zuzei. Chad gadya, chad gadya.

5 V'ata nura v'saraf l'chutra d'hika l'khalba d'nashakh l'shun'ra, d'akh'la l'gadya, d'zabin aba bitrei zuzei. Chad gadya, chad gadya.

6 V'ata maya v'khava l'nura, d'saraf l'chutra, d'hika l'khalba, d'nashakh l'shun'ra, d'akh'la l'gadya, d'zabin aba bitrei zuzei. Chad gadya, chad gadya.

7 V'ata tora v'shata l'maya, d'khava l'nura, d'saraf l'chutra, d'hika l'khalba, d'nashakh l'shun'ra, d'akh'la l'gadya, d'zabin aba bitrei zuzei. Chad gadya, chad gadya.

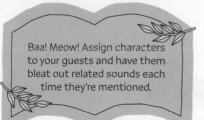

Baa! Meow! Assign characters to your guests and have them bleat out related sounds each time they're mentioned.

8 וְאָתָא הַשּׁוֹחֵט וְשָׁחַט לְתוֹרָא, דְּשָׁתָה לְמַיָּא,
דְּכָבָה לְנוּרָא, דְּשָׂרַף לְחוּטְרָא,
דְּהִכָּה לְכַלְבָּא, דְּנָשַׁךְ לְשׁוּנְרָא, דְּאָכְלָה לְגַדְיָא,
דְּזַבִּין אַבָּא בִּתְרֵי זוּזֵי. חַד גַּדְיָא, חַד גַּדְיָא.

9 וְאָתָא מַלְאַךְ הַמָּוֶת וְשָׁחַט לְשׁוֹחֵט, דְּשָׁחַט לְתוֹרָא,
דְּשָׁתָה לְמַיָּא, דְּכָבָה לְנוּרָא, דְּשָׂרַף לְחוּטְרָא,
דְּהִכָּה לְכַלְבָּא, דְּנָשַׁךְ לְשׁוּנְרָא, דְּאָכְלָה לְגַדְיָא,
דְּזַבִּין אַבָּא בִּתְרֵי זוּזֵי. חַד גַּדְיָא, חַד גַּדְיָא.

10 וְאָתָא הַקָּדוֹשׁ בָּרוּךְ הוּא וְשָׁחַט לְמַלְאַךְ הַמָּוֶת,
דְּשָׁחַט לְשׁוֹחֵט, דְּשָׁחַט לְתוֹרָא, דְּשָׁתָה לְמַיָּא,
דְּכָבָה לְנוּרָא, דְּשָׂרַף לְחוּטְרָא, דְּהִכָּה לְכַלְבָּא,
דְּנָשַׁךְ לְשׁוּנְרָא, דְּאָכְלָה לְגַדְיָא, דְּזַבִּין אַבָּא בִּתְרֵי זוּזֵי.
חַד גַּדְיָא, חַד גַּדְיָא.

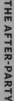

8 Then came the *shocheit* and slaughtered the bull, that drank up the water, that put out the fire, that burnt the stick, that hit the dog, that bit the cat, that ate the kid, that my father bought for two *zuz*, one kid, one kid.

9 Then came the angel of death and killed the *shocheit*, who slaughtered the bull, that drank up the water, that put out the fire, that burnt the stick, that hit the dog, that bit the cat, that ate the kid, that my father bought for two *zuz*, one kid, one kid.

10 Then came the Holy One and slew the angel of death, who killed the *shocheit*, who slaughtered the bull, that drank up the water, that put out the fire, that burnt the stick, that hit the dog, that bit the cat, that ate the kid, that my father bought for two *zuz*, one kid, one kid.

8 V'ata hashocheit v'shachat l'tora, d'shata l'maya, d'khava l'nura, d'saraf l'chutra, d'hika l'khalba, d'nashakh l'shun'ra, d'akh'la l'gadya, d'zabin aba bitrei zuzei. Chad gadya, chad gadya.

9 V'ata mal'akh hamavet v'shachat l'shocheit, d'shachat l'tora, d'shata l'maya, d'khava l'nura, d'saraf l'chutra, d'hika l'khalba, d'nashakh l'shun'ra, d'akh'la l'gadya, d'zabin aba bitrei zuzei. Chad gadya, chad gadya.

10 V'ata HaKadosh Barukh Hu v'shachat l'mal'akh hamavet, v'shachat l'shocheit, d'shachat l'tora, d'shata l'maya, d'khava l'nura, d'saraf l'chutra, d'hika l'khalba, d'nashakh l'shun'ra, d'akh'la l'gadya, d'zabin aba bitrei zuzei. Chad gadya, chad gadya.

Mazel tov!

Let's do it
again next year.

The Promised Land

Readings for
Beyond the Seder

ENOUGH ALREADY

By Howard Jacobson

If there were such a thing as a perfect Jewish joke, it might just be "Dayenu," the Passover punch line that is never enough.

One of the most enjoyable parts of the Passover ceremony is the singing, invariably full-throated in my experience, of all fifteen verses of "Dayenu":

> *Had he brought us out from Egypt, and not carried out judgments against them—Dayenu, it would have sufficed us! Had he carried out judgments against them, and not against their idols—it would have sufficed us! Had he destroyed their idols, and not smitten their first born, Dayenu . . .*
>
> *. . . Enough already!*

That, of course, though we thought our comical uncles blasphemous when they said it at the Seder table—"Enough already, when do we eat?"—is what the word "Dayenu" means. "It would have sufficed", "it would have been enough"; "we can imagine a point at which we would have been satisfied"—except that as a people we are never satisfied.

In the midst of gratitude, there is always a little something else we feel we have to ask for. Isn't this what "Dayenu" means? Hence the number of rogue, shopping-list "Dayenus" that spring up every day: feminist "Dayenus," gay "Dayenus," Zionist and anti-Zionist "Dayenus," even, I recall reading, a "Dayenu" praising the invasion of Iraq—"If He had destroyed the Ba'ath party idols, and not smitten Uday and Qusay—Dayenu, it would have been enough for us." The "Dayenu" is a please masquerading as a thank-you. We give thanks in order to ask for more.

We sing "Dayenu" at a solemn moment in the Seder service, soon after we have spilled a drop of wine from our glasses, one drop for each plague. It is a song of praise to the Almighty, thanking Him for our deliverance from slavery in Egypt and for the many gifts, including the Sabbath and the Torah, He bestowed upon us thereafter. As such, it is a spiritual high point of the service. Yet we sing it with immense gusto and, at many a Seder I've attended, mirth. A mirth that is over and above the pleasure we take in the inordinacy of God's munificence. Why? Because we know that we are making a great joke at our own expense.

Without doubt it is owing to God's bounty and protection that we are in a position to be making jokes at all. But, as with all good jokes, there is a whiff of terror in this one, too. How funny would it have been had God left the job half-done—and each verse pivots around a job half-done—how funny *will* it be when the things He doesn't do outweigh the things He does?

Could we say that this dread is no less psychological than historical? We fear abandonment. What happens when the giving stops?

The "Dayenu" is a series of self-generating conditional clauses, composed, if you like, in that most *kop-dreying* of all tenses, the Judaeo-hypothetic-preconditional, in which problems are imagined in advance of their occurring, imagined, indeed, in spite of their having been averted, and there is no fathoming the sequence of causation: Do our travails precede our giving thanks, or does our giving thanks occasion our travails? In one sense, our gratitude is forever playing catch-up with His infinite magnanimity; but in another—driven on by the rhythmic expectations of those clauses—it is we who are pushing Him to go on showering us with more favors.

Yet there is purpose in this nudging. Superfluous though we insist each of God's favors and blessings to us was, the truth is we would have been in serious trouble without any of them. For where would have been the use of His leading us to the Red Sea had He not parted it; or our wandering for forty years in the wilderness had He not provided us with manna? We say the one would have sufficed without the other, but in fact it would not. Thus the song is as much a rehearsal of complaints we might have voiced, and might voice yet, as it is a hymn of praise.

Built into this magnificent song of gratitude, therefore, is the fact of our colossal ingratitude. Nothing is enough for us. Not because we are vainglorious or greedy, but because our appetite for *intellectual* dissatisfaction, like our apprehension of disaster, knows no bounds. Call it the ravenousness of reasoning—the rabbinic "on the one hand this; on the other hand that." Call it our love of striking bargains. Call it hyperbole. Call it what you like, it is the bedrock of Jewish comedy. As it is the bedrock of our faith.

The Jewish joke is above all a strategy for survival. It looks, of necessity, to the future. It anticipates a woe before that woe is visited upon us. It gets in first with the criticism and the cruelty. If anybody is going to knock us around, it won't be the Cossacks, it will be ourselves. So that while a Jewish joke appears to be the perfecting of self-denigration, it is actually the opposite. It is the fruit of a perpetual vigilance and in the process demonstrates an intelligence that is, because it has to be, unremitting.

If there were such a thing as a perfect Jewish joke—and who is to say that the "Dayenu" is not it?—it would never finish. Ours is a religion of suspense. We wait and wait, for a God who cannot show Himself and a Messiah we would rather never came. We await an end, as we await a punch line, to a narrative that has no end. And just when we thought it was all over, it begins again. What are the last words of the "Dayenu"? "It would have sufficed us . . ." But by now our ear demands another clause, another gift, another setback for God to overcome. There is no final thank-you because there is no final sufficiency.

In this way, the grammar of "Dayenu" hovers on the edge of tragedy. Macbeth's numbed response to his wife's death—"There would have been a time for such a word"—gives us insight into how a conditional tense can turn a might-have-been into a cannot-any-longer-be. We can run out of feeling, as we can run out of hope. We can lose the words in which to express our own humanity. We, too, have been in Macbeth's position. We have supped full with horrors and believed that words will no longer—perhaps *should* no longer—come.

"Time present and time past are both perhaps present in time future," declaimed the Anglo-Catholic poet T. S. Eliot. Jewish time is more vertiginous still because of the element of joking we impart to it. "Oy, am I thirsty," cries the old Jewish man. "Oy, am I thirsty!" Alarmed bystanders give him a drink. Gratefully, he glugs it down. "Oy," he cries, "was I thirsty!"

Then and now change places in the absurd hyperbole of suffering. But at least to be able to say we were thirsty is a liberation, if not from the memory of thirst, then from thirst itself. This liberation is what the "Dayenu" commemorates. The comic repetition of "it would have sufficed us" asserts that there still is time for such a word, that it will go on sufficing whatever happens. In this, does it not epitomize the spirit of re-telling, re-making, and re-remembering that is the Passover itself?

ELIJAH

By Anne Roiphe

A tale of sin and redemption

There were two goats tethered to a tree on the slope leading to the temple. The people had come from their farms, from their villages, from the countryside, from the city. They were gathered with their families waiting for the sound of the shofar, for the end of the day of atonement, when they would pack up their baskets, carry sleeping children on their shoulders, and begin the year, the year that would soon arrive, a year in which once again their sins would repeat themselves, with new ones added in.

The goats were both white-haired with whiskers of black and tufts of black along their spines, over their haunches, and above their hooves. Their mouths closed over pink gums and teeth still white and slightly protruding. Their underbellies were taut with white hairs scattered here and there. Their ears were peaked and moved easily forward and back, listening without listening to the songs coming from the inner sanctum, the cries of babies and the babble of human voices that covered the approach to the temple itself. The goats inhaled the smoke from the small firepits nearby.

What can an animal know of time? Did the goats sense that as each minute passed, their lives were shortened—the wind on the back, the sun heating the ground, the taste of grain, the sweet smell of grass and weed, mole and dog, would disappear? Can a goat imagine the end of itself? Hopefully not. Hopefully as the chants in the inner temple went on and on, the goats had only goat thoughts of odors and the sounds of insects and the needs of the body, things that come in and things that go out. Sometimes there is sleep, and sometimes there is being, goat-being.

And also the other goat. The two had been born at the same time and knew no world without the other, the sound of the other, its bleat, its wool, its warmth on cold nights, its body always near, the sound of its hooves when they were moved from place to place. Even a goat knows it is better to be two rather than one, a fact of life that needs no explanation but is like the air and the rain and the grass underfoot, the way it is and so must always be.

The priests approached. They stood beside the goats. One was separated from his brother. There was a knife. It flashed in the last of the day's sunlight. The goat's throat opened, and blood splashed down on the grass, and the goat sank forward on his legs, and blood turned the ground red and the grass red, and the blood spattered upon the priests' robes. It was as it should be. Maybe quick, maybe death came before pain.

Watching the priests was a man with a bald head and a fringe of hair circling his head, which he held at a slightly cocked angle to his neck. He was not a priest. His robe was simple. His sandals worn thin with use. He watched as the priests picked up the other goat and pushed him down into the blood of his brother so that his fur was stained. The goat was afraid, and in his fear, he soiled the ground. The priests went on chanting. The goat rose to his feet and tried to get away, but a rope held him tightly in place.

A crowd of people pushed forward to see the remaining goat. Many of the men in the crowd had sticks in their hands. Soon the priest who held the rope that constrained the goat cut the rope and the goat bolted forward, where was he going, anywhere, anyway. The man in the crowd with the bald head fringed with long hair stayed near the goat as he ran toward the woods ahead. The crowd was cheering and shouting and throwing small stones at the goat. Some waved their sticks, and when the goat turned to go back, the men with sticks hit him and drove him forward.

What can a goat understand of this? A goat will only know to run, to try to escape the crowd of men, the voices, the sticks, the rocks. Deeper and deeper into the forest he went, and alongside him came the bald-headed man. He had no stick in his hand. He went with the goat forward, and down over the rocks, and into the woods, the long woods, thick with pine and dirt and darkness. The goat was afraid of the darkness, but when he turned up the slope he could hear the voices of the men with sticks, he could hear their shouts. He could hear their calls to each other.

Come, said Elijah to the goat. I'm here with you. Wait, said the goat. I'm tired. We need to go now, said Elijah. Who are you? said the goat. Your friend, said Elijah.

The goat moved forward until he was so tired he couldn't move anymore. He lay down, and Elijah sat down next to him. He stroked the goat's head. He cleaned the goat's fur with leaves that were floating in a nearby stream. The smell of blood is gone, said Elijah. Go to sleep, he told the goat, and the goat slept a long time.

While the goat was dreaming of blood and knives, a wolf appeared from under a bramble and tangle of fallen tree limbs and branches broken in a recent storm. The wolf looked at the goat. He bared his teeth. No, said Elijah, not this goat. The wolf stopped and looked at Elijah. He bared his teeth. I see a deer, said Elijah, behind the tree. He pointed down toward the valley, far down the mountainside. The wolf turned, ears forward, tail straight back, toward the rocks below.

When the goat woke, it was dark. Above the trees, the stars were floating in their constellations. The moon was full but the tall trees blocked its light and in the dark, the goat whimpered. He rose to his feet and wandered back and forth. His brother was gone. What is time to a goat? What is gone to a goat? Perhaps just the smell and the feel of the other's body, of the familiar heartbeat, the nuzzling of another mouth near the grain. What it meant to the goat was a long shiver, a sense that all was lost. The man beside him put his hands on the goat's head. Don't fear the dark, he said. I'm here with you.

The goat whimpered and shivered some more. You are in the woods, said Elijah. I am with you. My name is Elijah and I will stay with you awhile. And the goat moved next to the man and rubbed his fur against the wool robe the man had wrapped around himself. It would get colder as the night wore on. It would be a long night. Be near me, said the goat. I am, said Elijah.

And there was a low growl from behind the trees and the goat, who had once seen wolves attack the straggler in the flock even as the shepherd threw a rock at its head, let out a bleat, a bleat that sounded not unlike the dashes and dots of the shofar that he had heard as he was running into the woods. But the sounds that the goat made had no pattern, no power to reach the doors of heaven. The goat made goat sounds that might once have brought his goat mother to his side but now echoed aimlessly above his head. The wolf is back, said the goat. I know, said Elijah.

We are going to move, said Elijah, and he pushed the goat in front of him and the pair made their way forward deeper into the woods. The goat now recognized the size, the shape, the smell of Elijah and he moved forward in the dark, stumbling over the thick roots of high trees, kicking up dirt and anthills, and stepping on crickets and worms that crawled under the leaves, and Elijah led the goat toward the deepest part of the woods where the rocks were covered in moss and the branches formed a roof overhead and the animals of the woods sometimes paused to maul and devour their prey.

A goat can't think, why, what, what did I do to make them so angry with me? A goat can't imagine the heavy load of sins he was carrying on his back. But his heart can beat fast, and he knows fear and wonder.

He knows the surprise of the morning sun and the evening light and the smells of his flock and the quenching of his thirst in the brook and the feel of purple thistles and wildflowers as they brush past his legs. The goat knew in the dark to stay close to Elijah, the man who had appeared suddenly and sung to him as they moved down from the mountaintop, deeper and deeper into the darkness.

Elijah said to the goat when the goat stumbled and lay down, you're carrying the sins of the people away from the city, away from the villages, away from those who lied, who swore, who stole, who were selfish, who ignored the cries of the poor or turned their backs on their own children and dishonored their wives. The goat said, I don't understand. You are taking away their evil thoughts and their bad deeds, said Elijah, but what could this mean to a goat, though it meant everything to the howling mob at the mountaintop? I don't understand, said the goat. I know, said Elijah.

Elijah sat down at the base of a tree, and the goat came and put his head in Elijah's lap. Elijah was not sorry that the goat had no idea of good and evil, not in the world and not in himself. He envied the goat his innocence. In a nearby tree, an owl hooted. Deeper into the forest, there was a roar of an animal, a jackal perhaps. I promise you, said Elijah to the goat, I will not leave you tonight.

Why, thought Elijah, would God want the slaughter of an innocent animal? Did God actually eat? Why, thought Elijah, would God ask Abraham for the death of his only son? In the dark of the forest with the goat beside him, Elijah thought of God, God the cruel, God the devouring, God the creator who drowned His creation, who brought flood and famine and disease, who punished even before the crime was committed. God, thought Elijah, is the Great Murderer. In a forest, late at night when the moon can hardly be seen between the thick branches above, when the warm body of the goat pressed against his legs, Elijah thought less of God than was proper. But there is no need to be proper in the dark wood.

Above the trees, the wind was blowing. It was coming out of the west and the leaves rustled frantically and the current in the brook beat at the rocks that stood alongside the moving waters. The fish went down to the bottom as far as they could go. The birds took shelter against the trunks of the trees and the goat felt fear again. Elijah found shelter behind a fallen bush and the goat smelled the damp of the earth. The wind picked up strength and the goat pushed against Elijah's legs until he put his arms around the goat and held him against his chest as the wind whipped about. On the temple mount, the priests were pleased that the storm had come after the day had ended and all had gone as it should and as they believed it would go until the end of time.

And so the night passed; the floor of the forest was dark with the waters that had fallen out of the sky, been shaken from the leaves of the trees, had risen from the fullness of the river that flowed downward from the mountaintop toward the distant sea.

It was the day after the goat had lost his brother, and the goat was already beginning to forget that once he woke to the smell and the warm fur of the other, and once he was not a singular goat but a part of the flock. Once he had not known the man who was now by his side. Now he did. This was not a puzzle for the goat. It was simply the way it was. Perhaps it is better to be a goat than to be a man.

The pair made their way through the tangle of branches. The wind had blown down saplings and leaves scattered everywhere and the rocks that protruded out of the dirt were large and there was no path, no route, just a struggle forward. Elijah sang and the goat walked. His whiskers were still stained with small drops of the blood of his brother, and his body carried the smell of his brother.

No longer could they hear the rock-throwing men, the stick-waving men at the mount. There was a chirping of insects, the calling of birds, and the darkness and the smell of moss and dung and the buzzing of insects in and out of the ears of Elijah and his goat.

They reached a ravine that led to a rivulet of running water far below and a sharp drop downward. The goat stopped. Elijah heard the wings of a large bird and looked up. An owl sat on the branch. What have you got? the owl asked Elijah. The scapegoat, answered Elijah, he's carrying the sins of the people away from the city, away from the farms, away from the sinners. That little goat? said the owl. Ha, said the owl. Don't the people know that one day they will be the goats carried away into the unknown and that others will beat them with sticks and welcome them with knives and they themselves will carry the sins of the people? Ha, said the owl, the stupidity!

They're doing the best they can, said Elijah. Ha, said the owl. They don't know what is going to happen, the dolts. How can they know? said Elijah. Their future is a secret because it hasn't come yet. They don't know much more than this poor goat. But I know, said the owl, and then he repeated himself. I know. Soon the whole nation will be the scapegoat for their own sins, they will be driven away from their home and in the new places they go, they will see what it means to be beaten, to pay for the sins of others. Ha, said the owl, they will see.

He saw a small rodent behind the bush near the goat and with a swoop of his large wings and a quick opening of his claws, he picked it up and returned to his branch with his prey. You want some? he asked Elijah. No thank you, Elijah said. You? asked the owl of the goat. The goat did not answer. Suit yourself, said the owl.

What are you going to do with that goat, said the owl. Stay with him, said Elijah. How nice you are, said the owl, a romantic, a sentimental teary fool who will amuse the children once a year, what a joke you are, you can't prevent the people from turning into goats sent into the wilderness and you can't even save this one goat. Can I have a piece when you are done? asked the owl. You take what you can, said Elijah. I will, said the owl. A little big for me, but I'll get a small part, maybe a liver. I don't like that owl, said the goat. I know, said Elijah.

A mist fell from the sky over the trees, drifted down toward the brown earth, covered fallen branches, bare logs, wet the wings of insects, made the goat stumble forward. Elijah made himself a staff and pushed ahead slowly. There was no path, there was no direction but up and down and Elijah and his companion were going down. The goat was afraid and between each step he paused. Elijah picked him up and brought him across the stones or over the tree limb and across the hole that was in their way. The goat's fur was wet. A half circle of spiderweb hung from his haunches. From a distance there came an angry call from a jackal on the hunt. The goat quivered. He understood the sound the way a child understands a hand raised to slap an upturned face. Don't worry, said Elijah.

The goat could smell Elijah even when the mist was so thick he couldn't see him. Elijah could hear the goat breathing behind him. They made their way to the edge of a gorge, a sharp drop of rocks that led down to the slender stream of water below. The day had reached its midpoint. Elijah picked some berries from a bush and sat down to eat them. The goat nibbled at some grass and lay at Elijah's feet. The sun was breaking through the clouds and suddenly rays of light drifted down through the branches of the trees and there was a golden color around the gorge and a pale light rested on leaf and bush, on the sap-stained pine needles, on the dark still-drying earth. Sparrows and starlings took flight and rose above the treetops.

It may as well be here, Elijah thought. He sat on the high rock above the running water and he called to the goat, who came to his side. I can't take you any farther, he said. He rubbed the goat's ears. Elijah put his face into the goat's neck. He took a deep breath. The goat was not afraid as long as Elijah's hand was on him. The goat had forgotten his brother and the shepherd and the fields of his home. After all, he was just a goat.

For a long time, Elijah didn't move. The goat was still, waiting for Elijah to rise and continue along the way. The goat didn't ask where they were going, or why they were going, or what lay ahead. He was just a goat selected at random, a perfect goat, no scars, no sores, no runny eyes, a perfect goat.

Elijah knew there would be other forests, other trenches, the sounds of guns at the backs of the people, other bodies fallen in the dirt one on top of another. Elijah tried not to know the things he knew about forests and dirt and limbs. And he picked the goat up in his arms. The goat was large enough so that it was hard to hold him, his legs thrashing in the air, and he held the goat out over the rocks and sang him a song that quieted the animal who rested in his arms and then with his eyes shut, Elijah moved to the edge of the ravine and dropped the goat, who fell, flailing his legs as if they could turn into wings, down to the river below onto the stones in that narrow river, onto the wet rocks that caused small rapids to rush forward, foam, and roar and all. Elijah saw the blood of the goat as it spilled into the running water and disappeared downstream. He saw the body of the goat half in the water and half on a rock, slipping now down toward the current that would carry the body away.

The owl flew low overhead. He was headed straight down toward the goat's body, his beak opened, his claws ready. A little bit of liver is all I want, he said to Elijah as he passed him by.

Elijah thought to himself, I kept him company. I eased his fear, I let him lean on me. I carried him. It was better than his being alone in this wood and dying with sharp teeth in his flank, or claws in his belly, or a snake around his throat. He died quickly. You don't say Kaddish for a goat, but there was a tenderness in Elijah that was itself a Kaddish that was both praise of the Lord and criticism of His ways.

There will be another goat next year, said Elijah to himself so he wouldn't lament beyond what was reasonable for the little goat whose life had been shortened so the people could feel pure.

And then Elijah disappeared.

MY SONG

By Anthony Mordechai Tzvi Russell

As a black classical singer,
I avoided singing negro
spirituals—until Yiddish
music helped me hear them
in a new way as a Jew.

The first time I heard a live rendition of "Go Down, Moses" was at
the first Passover Seder I ever attended. Somewhere around the third
cup of wine, a room full of Jews sang the classic negro spiritual in
lively fashion, followed almost immediately by "O Freedom," another
classic negro spiritual.

A feeling of bewilderment and paranoia began to steal over me:
Why are they singing these songs? Are they looking at me? Do they
expect me to know these songs?

That was before I converted. Now that I've formally been a Jew
for a few years, being the only black man in Jewish spaces has lost
some of its initial awkwardness. Still, at that first Seder, I was my
own source of awkwardness. I wouldn't say I'd been actively running
away from negro spirituals, but I'd spent fifteen years as an African
American classical singer scrupulously avoiding singing them. That
Seder was indeed a "night of questions," implicated as I was by the
question of the Wicked Child: What does all this mean to you?

I struggled to retain my cool. This is Passover, I told myself. A
time to sing songs about Moses. A time to sing songs about freedom.
This, for once, is really not about you.

Or was it? That question would be eventually answered by
another question—in Yiddish.

Despite the fact that my family's roots in the Church of Christ lie
geographically close to the sources of the negro spiritual, I grew up
in the Bay Area, where religious music—Christian and Jewish—is
influenced as much by modern rock, folk, and world music as it is by
its own traditions. Church might have been one of the last places I
would have heard a spiritual as a child.

My first encounters with negro spirituals came instead when
I began training as a classical singer in the late '90s, when I was

seventeen. Spirituals are a defining feature of black classical singers, from Paul Robeson to Jessye Norman. It is something of an unspoken rule that singers of color should devote at least part of their recital and recording repertoire to spirituals—at the very least, choosing a spiritual as an encore after having sung over an hour's worth of high-toned European music.

When I began my training, I knew immediately that I didn't want to be so easily defined by something as obvious as my race. I chose a repertoire of mostly Mozart, some Handel, a little Verdi, and a little Brahms. I sang a diverse variety of roles; playing a Spanish gardener in an Italian opera by an Austrian composer based on a French play was just the tip of the iceberg. After concert performances, however, oftentimes audience members would express their disappointment that I had failed to burst into the rendition of "Ol' Man River" they felt I had owed them as an African American bass.

I went on in the fall of 2007 to make my professional opera debut in the world premiere of Philip Glass's Civil War–era *Appomattox* with the San Francisco Opera Company. It was in the role of a freed slave, so obviously my attempts to transcend race hadn't worked very well, but this role was different. In the opera I ran out to meet Abraham Lincoln and, to the strains of Glass's glorious music, I sang him Psalm 47—not a spiritual, exactly, but decidedly not "Ol' Man River."

Listening in the audience was my boyfriend of barely two months, Michael Rothbaum, a rabbi I had met that summer in New York. Almost as soon as the curtain dropped on *Appomattox*, I moved across the country to be with him, formally converting to Judaism three years later at Congregation Sons of Israel, a conservative shul in Nyack, New York.

Becoming a Jew meant being defined by choice: the deliberate acceptance of texts, narratives, tropes, and experiences that would now inform my view of the world. Becoming a classical singer had also involved the acceptance of texts and experiences—from learning how to watch a conductor out of the corner of my eye to memorizing late-nineteenth-century German poetry—though to completely different ends. After fifteen years, I grew weary of the competition, rejection, technical difficulties, great expense, and casual racism I found in the world of classical singing. I left the stage in October 2011.

Having just fled the stage, I tried to find a new direction in the texts, narratives, and experiences I had chosen to accept as a Jew. These, in turn, led me to those sounds I had carefully tried to avoid. They led me to myself.

> In dem land fun piramidn
> Geven a kenig, beyz un shlekht
> Zenen dort geven di yidn
> Zayne diner, zayne knekht. . . .

In the land of the pyramids
There was a king, angry and evil
There, the Jews were
His servants, his slaves. . . .

Thus ran "Piramidn," the first song I ever learned in Yiddish, just a month after leaving the stage. Coming from a classical background, I was not particularly impressed with it. The melody was simple and the words by anarchist poet David Edelstadt seemed too didactic for any kind of effective "artistic" interpretation.

The first time I heard a live rendition of "Piramidn" was also at a Seder, where it suddenly made profound sense. The song not only told the narrative of Passover but moved its message into the present: "Folk, ver vet dikh haynt bafrayen?"—"People, who will free you today?"

It may come as a surprise that I—a youngish African American gay convert—have any affinities with the world of Yiddish song. But right there, at the beginning of my Yiddish journey, was a story I could credibly portray. I knew the discontents of a history that included "di viste shklafnvelt," "the bleak slavery-world" described in "Piramidn."

I began to take on the repertoire of Sidor Belarsky, one of the twentieth century's most prolific performers of cantorial music, Hasidic nigunim, and Yiddish art song. Gaining an entirely new repertoire, I tried it out for the first time performing a short concert in Yiddish one afternoon in January 2012 at the Sholem Aleichem Kultur Tsenter in the Bronx.

In Yiddish, I began to find texts with arresting parallels to my own dim recollections of the spirituals I had so cavalierly rejected at the beginning of my career. Spirituals suddenly became something different; I could allow myself to hear them with different ears from the ones that heard "Go Down, Moses" years earlier at my first Seder. I could now hear my own history along with striking projections, elaborations, and celebrations of the foundational texts I had accepted as a part of myself as a Jew.

When I made the choice to become Jewish, I wasn't expecting to find my own experiences, personal and inherited, to be trebled so closely by aspects of Jewish culture. I eventually remembered what partially led me to Judaism in the first place: my deep love for the narratives, phrases, and images of the Jewish scriptures, disseminated to me as an African American child of religious upbringing.

I have become fascinated with the appropriation of foundational images and texts from Judaism that have become integral to African American religious expression. How can I begin to convey the resonance of phrases like "My Rock, in whom there is no flaw" (Psalm 92) when that euphonious phrase falls upon the African American religious heart and mind, held there as surely as "light is stored up for the righteous"? The cultural or artistic use of music that is tied to a particular historical moment can be moving in its ability to transcend space and time.

The meaning of these traditional African American texts to me as a Jew—to me, and not necessarily to you, to paraphrase the Haggadah—has become intensely personal, nuanced, and idiosyncratic. I haven't necessarily lost all of the bewilderment I felt hearing "Go Down, Moses" at my first Seder.

I can't help wondering if I will throw my voice wholeheartedly behind any spirituals I may happen to hear over the Seder table this year. Most likely I will. If you should happen to hear my voice, know that it will be for reasons that are specific instead of general, acquired instead of assumed: I am remembering my own past as I perform the mitzvah of the Seder in the present. I am present at the Seder table as I enrich the meaning of these mitzvahs in my future.

Acknowledgments

A Haggadah is always, by definition, a group effort, with one generation continuing the work where others left off. This Haggadah was brought to life by *Tablet* magazine, spearheaded by Alana Newhouse, Stephanie Butnick, and Liel Leibovitz.

Many of the texts and translations in this Haggadah come courtesy of two excellent open-source resources, Haggadot.com and Sefaria.org. They have our gratitude, as does Eve Lavavi, whose song translations appear here. Thanks to Daniel Tabak for the Hebrew translation work, and Gideon Klionsky and Rachel Rosenthal for the transliteration.

At Artisan, we were led through the wilderness by Lia Ronnen, Shoshana Gutmajer, Zach Greenwald, Nina Simoneaux, Carson Lombardi, and Nancy Murray. Many thanks as well to Jin Auh and Alexandra Christie at the Wylie Agency. *Tablet*'s publisher, Morton Landowne, embodies the best and rarest values of Jewish leadership.

And finally, we are eternally grateful to the writers and artists whose contributions, old and new, are featured in this Haggadah: Liz Galst, Jordana Horn Gordon, Wayne Hoffman, Leah Koenig, Howard Jacobson, MaNishtana, Daphne Merkin, Tova Mirvis, Louis Nayman, Abigail Pogrebin, Anne Roiphe, Anthony Mordechai Tzvi Russell, Andrea Sparacio, and Marc Tracy.

About the Artist

Born in Israel in 1971, Shai Azoulay lives and works in Jerusalem. He received both his BFA and MFA from the Bezalel Academy of Art and Design Jerusalem.

Azoulay's works have been exhibited around the world, including in shows in New York, London, Tokyo, Paris, and Rome. In 2011, Azoulay had his first major museum show at the Tel Aviv Museum of Art. His work was featured at Frieze Art Fair in London and is included in major private and public collections.

About *Tablet* Magazine

Founded in 2009, *Tablet* is a daily outlet covering news, culture, religion, and more and has published a line of books with Artisan that includes *The 100 Most Jewish Foods: A Highly Debatable List* (2019) and *The Newish Jewish Encyclopedia: From Abraham to Zabar's and Everything in Between* (2019). Its weekly podcast, *Unorthodox*, is the number one Jewish podcast on iTunes.